Fin \,

Afikoman

Encountering Jesus in the Spring Feasts

*When I found the one I love
I held him and would not let him go*
Song of Solomon 3:4

Christie Eisner

Ruth's Road

PO Box 481131 • Kansas City • Missouri • 64148

Scripture quotations are from the New King James Version of the Bible unless otherwise specified. All scriptures quoted are set in a different font from the rest of text; all emphases added are mine. Copyright 1979,1980, 1982, Thomas Nelson, Inc., Publisher.

Edited by: Jessica Bouzianis

Cover design: RaDean Mynatt

Ruth's Road Logo: Abigail Eisner

ISBN: 0692498737
ISBN-13: 978-0692498736 (Ruth's Road)

~ Dedication ~

Dedicated to our children Ben, Emmy and Sarah who I love and value with all my heart.

Also to our four beautiful granddaughters, Elizabeth, Abigail, Emma, and baby June… My delight, my treasures… I write down the "words of this life" and pray that you will find Jesus, the Pearl of great price, and love Him with all your hearts… and that someday, this book will help you to love Him more.

~ In Fond Memory of Omi ~

This journey would never have begun without my mother-in-law Hildegard Eisner, known to our family as "Omi". She was a little 4'6" "powerhouse" that taught me so much about life that it would be a book in itself to write it all down. She and her husband Bernard were Jewish holocaust survivors. They escaped from Germany in 1939 and found refuge for nine years in Shanghai, China. After losing their German homeland, family, and friends to the Nazis under Adolf Hitler, she and Bernard came to the United States in 1949. They had $15.00 in their pocket, a 4-year-old daughter, and she was pregnant with my husband, John. She was a true survivor in every way, and an example of how to live life to its fullest by refusing to be a victim of her past.

She loved her kids and grandchildren, and her love language was food. "Eat, eat, you look so hungry!", she would say when you came in her house. And, hungry or not, you had no choice but to eat! There was always chicken soup bubbling on her stove and she would hover around making sure that everything in her refrigerator was offered at least 10 times! She would be proud to know that she has mentored me well. Our kids always comment when visiting, "Your refrigerator looks like Omi's!"

Being a Gentile, I was initially not the daughter-in-law she would have chosen for her son, and when he and I became Christians in 1975 our relationship was strained for a while. However, in time, love won, like it often does. Between Omi refusing to live in bitterness and my persistence to be loved and accepted by her, we became very close friends. One of my favorite feelings when going to her house was her excitement she showed when I walked through the door. "My Christie!!" she would say in an excited voice as she came to greet me. Such a simple gesture always healed something in my soul because I knew she was truly happy to see me.

She will never know the value and the richness she added to my life. I am not even sure I can put into words what those things are; I am just deeply aware that knowing her made me a better person. There is a Jewish concept called "tikun olam" that is part of the Jewish mindset. It means, to "repair the world", to live your life leaving the world a better place than you found it. I, for one, am a more whole person for having been in Omi's life. She was a legend that lives on in all of us who were privileged enough to know her.

~ In Honor of Tim Ruthven ~

John and I met Tim Ruthven, our spiritual father, in 1982. Tim was a missionary to America from New Zealand and was sent by God to strengthen the hearts of believers into an intimate, daily relationship with God in His Word. Tim's teaching series, called "That I might Know Him", was a four-part teaching about Tim's personal encounters with Jesus, and his teaching, made me hungry to have a relationship like that for myself. I asked Tim what I could do to know Him like he did and he answered, "Get an alarm clock." He said that the way to intimacy was to set your alarm clock every morning and to start your day with a daily reading plan, going through the Bible every year. He said, "That way, if God has something to say to me, He knows where to find me." It sounded a bit religious and legalistic to me at first, but the fruit in Tim's life and the adventures and encounters he had with God for many years were far from religious! Now 33 years later, I am glad I listened to him and can honestly say that the result is boxes full of journals filled with personal history with Jesus. When Tim died in 2006, we lost a friend, a father in the faith and a faithful friend of God. I am so thankful for all that he taught us, not just with words but in the way he lived his life.

My favorite teaching of Tim's was on the book of Ruth. In his thick New Zealand accent, Tim would teach about how "little Ruth," a Moabite girl, followed her Jewish mother-in-law to Bethlehem Judah. Bethlehem Judah, meaning "house of bread" and "house of praise", was where Ruth married Boaz, her Jewish bridegroom and kinsman-redeemer. I loved how Tim unfolded the love story found in the Book of Ruth and how he related it to being a type and shadow of a Gentile girl being joined to a Jewish bridegroom that brought redemption and the future Messiah. I always thought that if I could change my name, I would want to be called Ruth because I so loved this tender story.

One night, while in the process of writing this book, I felt the Lord call me "little Ruth", and then it hit me! It *is* my story! Like Ruth, I married a Jewish man, John, and his mother became my "Naomi"! (The name we called her was Omi!) I was her friend and daughter-in-law for thirty-three years and became familiar with and immersed in her Jewish community. As I gleaned in a Jewish field and learned the Jewish roots of my faith, ***"her God became my God and her people, my people" (Ruth 1:16)***. Clinging to this new heritage that I married into, I grew to understand the richness of the Hebraic culture of Jesus my Bridegroom. I followed "Ruth's road" and received a rich inheritance that I am now sharing with others.

In 2007 when Omi passed away at the age of 99, God spoke this verse from the Book of Ruth to my heart,

> *"And Boaz answered and said to her, "It has been fully reported to me, all that you have done for your mother-in-law... and how you have left your father and your mother and the land of your birth, and have come to a people whom you did not know before. The LORD repay your work, and a full reward be given you by the LORD God of Israel, under whose wings you have come for refuge."*
>
> *Ruth 2:11-12*

.

~ *Acknowledgments* ~

Hands down, at the top of my list, is my husband John, who knows "that I am but dust", but treats me like gold! Without him, I would not have this story to tell. He is my first Jewish bridegroom who, because of his heritage, introduced me to my eternal Jewish Bridegroom.

John has loved me, supported me, believed in me and has gone on this journey with me even when it was really hard to see where it was all going. We have been married for 40 years and I think the number one thing that has made our marriage and life together so good was something that happened to us on a hike the second year of our marriage when we were brand new believers. We were on our favorite trail near Allenspark, Colorado, standing by a river holding hands. As we stood there in silence, watching the rushing water pour over the rocks, we both came to the same realization at the same time: we were not equipped to do life.

We both absolutely knew, without ever having a conversation about it, that we were, as John put it, "groomed for failure". We were unskilled, college dropouts from the 70's and pregnant with our son, Ben. All of a sudden John broke the silence and prayed. He said, "We are trying to look like responsible adults, but God, You know the truth. We are two helpless, messed up kids that have no idea what we are doing. If you don't walk with us and help us do life, we will not make it. Please help us."

Now, forty years later I can testify to the power of that prayer. He has totally covered for us. He blessed our lives abundantly with everything we needed and more. He gave us a livelihood, three healthy kids, four grandkids (and counting), amazing spiritual mentors, a supportive extended family, rich friendships worldwide, and best of all, a personal relationship with the King and Creator of the universe! John and I know with certainty that we are totally, 100% as dependent on Him today as we were that day at the river.

There is a verse from Deuteronomy that sums it up well. Moses gives the children of Israel his "bottom line" priorities he hopes they will live by: ***"That you may love the LORD your God, that you may obey His voice, and that you may cling to Him, for He is your life and the length of your days." (Deut. 30:20)***. We are still clinging, and John and I feel that our real adventures together and with the Lord are just beginning!

**"We're holding on to your divine love
We're holding on and we're not letting go
It's not our zeal, it's that your love is strong,
It's not our faith, it's that You're faithful"
Jon Thurlow**

I want to thank our friends over the years; first our small groups in Colorado who encouraged us, strengthened us, and endured my blind passion for finding Jesus in the feasts of the Lord. Not knowing what I was doing or where it was leading, these small groups were the community we did life with, and naturally were the "guinea pigs" I practiced on! I am also so thankful for the close friends God has given us in Kansas City. What a rich community of sold out lovers of Jesus, faithful prayer partners and friends that God has given us for the journey. Life only works with community, and God has been faithful to give us friends to run with.

I am so thankful for my "study buddies", looking for the richness of our Hebrew roots together: My husband John, Jess and Alice, Eudis, Liz, Sarah, Kelli, Linda, Matt and Christina, and Daniel... I cannot believe we now have three sukkahs in our neighborhood to go "sukkah hopping" each year during the Feast of Tabernacles! You all made me realize that I did not make this stuff up; it is real, it is scriptural, and worth pursuing. We are no longer alone on this journey of looking for Jesus in the festivals and it is getting more exciting every day.

Jessica Bouzianis: Thank you for your long hours editing and helping us in so many ways. In spite of your busy life with three small children, you have given us endless hours of your valuable time and have served and encouraged me in so many ways. You even learned to interpret my thoughts in spite of my constant run-on sentences and were able to suggest changes without removing my heart. I also want to acknowledge your husband, Steven, who believed in this book and invested his time in various ways. Thank you, both, so much!!!

Daniel Schuman Kemp... In some odd way I will always be thankful that you hurt your knee because it forced you to have to take a sitting job at the welcome desk with me! The only reason I am typing this right now is because you believed in me and gave value to what I teach. John did too, but he and I are too much alike. We have passion but lack the initiative it takes to do more than just talk about things. You are the spark, the catalyst that makes things happen! I value the uncanny gift you have that communicates life into the gifts inside of others. I am actually fascinated watching it at work. You have a way of taking an embryo idea that can randomly come out of my mouth, and you validate and speak life into it, actually making it sound exciting! You make me sign up for my own ideas! How does that work?

I love the supernatural way that God crosses destinies in people's lives. Your friendship is a valuable gift to John and I, and somehow God got you to sign up with our "Ma and Pa adventure". I will never forget the night at our dinner table that we kind of mumbled our little idea to put my teaching onto paper and/or videos some time in the future. You immediately yelled, "I'm in! This is what I am supposed to do!" John and I were surprised at your excitement and kind of felt sorry for you having such a puny vision for your life. Not that we did not want you to be part of what we were doing; we just had a much higher vision for what you were capable of! But as it has unfolded, we are now seeing that without you, this would still be just a good idea that John and I discuss over coffee. We honor your heart that is passionate for the things on God's heart, we honor your gifts that are motivating, and in the end, bring honor and glory to Him by bringing His plans to birth so He can receive the reward in those He loves. You are a fellow "freak" and have a great testimony to prove it, and we love that God joined us with someone who not only gets us, but also can lead our parade!

I also want to acknowledge Mike Bickle at the International House of Prayer, who has blessed John and I for years; has fed and sustained our hearts with the pearls of wisdom and teaching that only a man who walks close to the heart of Jesus can know. Though not trying to put him on a pedestal, which he would not like, he is truly the best example of what a humble man of God looks like that we have ever seen. Mike's teaching on bridal love and studying the emotions of God in the Bible has been life changing for me. He once shared a powerful encounter that he had with the Lord when God told him, "Be patient, young man!" Mike explained that by "patient", the Lord was saying, "your assignment is for the long haul. Don't quit!" His perseverance, steadiness, consistency and sold out devotion to Jesus is an encouragement to the body of Christ worldwide. I remember a pastor from England who was visiting IHOPKC saying to me, "When I feel like quitting, I turn on the prayer room webstream and when I see Mike Bickle in there, still faithful to his calling after all these years, I say, if Mike can keep going, then I will too!" John and I, like many others, will always be grateful to have an example of what it looks like to be "a faithful witness".

Table of Contents

~ Preface ~

I never in a million years thought that the things I have carried in my heart about the biblical festivals would ever become a book. God tricked me. I say that very reverently but it is true.

I started on this journey in 1975 as a new believer. He caught me totally off guard by inconveniently showing up in the middle of a Passover meal at my Jewish in-law's house, and has been revealing Jesus to me in His feasts ever since. I never desired to be a scholar or an expert on this subject; in fact, most of the things He revealed to me over the years were hidden away in journals and were intimate secrets between He and I that have been vulnerable for me to share. I have been fascinated with the person of Jesus since the day I first met Him and have just always had a burning desire to encounter Him and to intimately know Him. I was not satisfied with knowledge about Him second hand. I wanted Him to personally show me the things in the Bible "concerning Himself" (Luke 24:27). In the 70's we were called "Jesus freaks" and I guess I still am. I just cannot find anything else in this world that is more pleasurable than knowing Him.

1

What I thought was just a personal journey of encountering Him in the Leviticus 23 feasts has now become a fast growing hunger in believers all over the world. I made a deal with God in 2008 when He first asked me to start sharing what I had learned from Him. I agreed to start sharing my story and the revelations that He showed me, but He had to send the people that were hungry to know. I would not go seeking places and people to share it with. And He did. One by one, group by group, and not just locally but from across the nations, He sent people with open hearts. John and I have crazy stories of how the Lord connected us with people from all over the world. When they stay at our house and a conversation opens up where they "ask the questions", I keep my bargain with God and share my heart.

What I have to share is more than information about the biblical festivals. Rather, I believe He has given me revelation of His divine love story that is hidden in the ceremonies and customs of the feasts and the Jewish culture that He expressed Himself in. I have discovered the language of these feasts hidden throughout the entire Old and New Testaments in the Bible. The information is important in understanding the rich inheritance that we were grafted into when we were born again. The Hebrew roots of our faith unlock mysteries and understanding that we have been blinded to for 1800 years.

God has asked me to write down and share what He has revealed to me over the years, mainly to serve as an invitation for others to encounter Him in the pattern of the festivals and to get their hearts strengthened by the revelation that the Bible is the greatest love story ever told. Simple as it may sound to theological minds, it really is all about a wedding!

In the first few chapters I am going to share my testimony of how I started searching for Jesus in the biblical festivals. I will then lay a foundation of Hebraic thought and philosophy that have run through the Jewish culture for thousands of years. It is necessary that I do this in order to give the feasts of the Lord context and meaning. I am also hoping to give greater understanding of what Gentile believers have been grafted into when we come to believe in the Jewish Messiah. My prayer is that you will receive fresh revelation of Jesus as you read this book and that you will be as amazed as I was to discover God's blueprint of how He is going to come to earth to redeem His bride. However, if all you are left with when you are done is a burning heart that loves Jesus more, then my assignment will be a success and He will be pleased.

~ Chapter 1 ~

The Journey Begins

*"Faith is not the clinging to a shrine but
an endless pilgrimage of the heart."*
Abraham Joshua Heschel

In 1974 when my husband John and I were a newly, happily married couple, I saw my first glimpse of his prophetic gift that burst my little "Pollyanna" bubble. He came in the door one day and almost angrily proclaimed, "If God is real then we need to do something more than just acknowledge He exists!" I thought to myself, "who does he think he is telling me there is something wrong with what and how I believe; besides, I don't even remember having this conversation!" But it was a true word from God that cut through my heart and set a drastic, life-long change into motion.

Soon after that day we were invited to go to a home church on the University of Colorado campus. The pastor was teaching from the book of John about a Man named

Jesus. In all of my 25 years, I had never opened a Bible, and Jesus was just a baby in the manger at Christmas. The more the pastor talked about Him, the more fascinated I became and I left there that night hungry to know more. As we returned each week I didn't realize I was becoming a Christian; I didn't know I was lost. I didn't come to Him initially as a guilty sinner; I came to Him because I fell in love with Him and told Him I wanted to know everything I could about Who He was. I related to Peter and the disciples when *Luke 5:11* says, *"They left all and followed".* That is exactly what happened to John and I. Jesus won our hearts and I was marked with the cry of Paul in *Philippians 3:10, "Oh that I might know Him"!* There was no other choice but to follow Him, like Abraham, not knowing where we were going.

It was in this mindset of *"diligently seeking Him" (Heb. 11:6),* that I stumbled into Jesus hidden in the biblical feasts. This is the journey I would like to invite you into as I share my testimonies and revelations that span over four decades of mining for gold that I found buried in the Leviticus 23 pattern of redemption. If you are only interested in information, you will miss the heart of this book. But if you are looking to understand the culture and family that Romans 11:17 says we're grafted into, and possibly encounter the heart of your Jewish Bridegroom, you might want to come along. It is a journey that will satisfy your desire for solid understanding of the scriptures and hopefully strengthen your heart to love Him more.

Our Background

When I married John in 1974, the fact that he was Jewish and I was not meant nothing to us. It did, however, mean something to John's family. Both his father and mother were Holocaust survivors. They escaped Germany in 1939 and found refuge in Shanghai, China for nine years before immigrating to the United States. Sadly, all of their remaining family members died in Hitler's concentration camps. Consequently, it was extremely important to them that John, being the only son to carry on their family name, observe Jewish traditions and marry within his faith. Needless to say they did not welcome me, a Gentile, into the family with excitement and open arms. Everyone knows that if you marry a Gentile they will cause your son or daughter to convert to Christianity. Well I knew that was not a problem because I was not a Christian either, and I assured John's mother that because I had no religion other than a generic belief in a higher power, she did not need to worry about me influencing her son in the area of religion!

My first meeting with John's parents was a bit shocking. What had I gotten myself into? His parents were short, European people with a thick German accent and a strange religion. They looked like they had stepped out of another century and I felt like I had been dropped onto another planet. The first time I went to their house for dinner I didn't know the "rules" and I felt like such a Gentile! I worked hard to make them love and accept me, and I knew John's mother lived with the hope of me converting to Judaism. Then a year after John and I were married, "God forbid", her worst nightmare happened. We became Christians!!! She was understandably upset, so to

appease her we agreed to go to her rabbi to be
"deprogrammed".

The Jews for Jesus movement, under a man named
Moshe Rosen, had headquarters in Denver, Colorado
where we were living. All the rabbis in town were warning
their congregations that he was after their children;
therefore the rabbi that we were sent to was very well
prepared with an intellectual argument of why Jesus could
not possibly be the Jewish Messiah. I remember being so
impressed with this man and his great wealth of knowledge.
We sat and listened for quite awhile as he took us through
the Old Testament. He even shared his knowledge of the
New Testament, explaining why it was a different religion.
His arguments were wasted on us. John and I had just
begun reading our Bibles and all we had was the simple
revelation that Jesus died for our sins. I only knew that a
Person named Jesus had encountered me and my life had
been turned upside down as a result. I could not tell anyone
why I believed what I did other than, like the blind man in
the book of John who was asked to explain to the religious
leaders how Jesus had healed him said, "all I know is that I
was blind and now I see".

When the rabbi was finally done with his argument
he put his pencil down, exasperated with our lack of
response, looked at us and said, "Ok, tell me, why do you
believe this stuff?" It was quiet as I searched my heart for a
minute and then told him the only answer that I had:
"Because God told me it was true." In an offended tone of
disbelief he asked, "God speaks to you?" I was quite
confused at his question, thinking that if God spoke to me
then surely He spoke to this rabbi who was so
knowledgeable! I answered in a sheepish voice, "Yes,
doesn't He speak to you?" With great annoyance and

frustration he got up from his chair, said he had nothing more to say to us, and showed us the door. Years later I realized the truth of the scripture, that God often chooses the foolish to confound the wise and uneducated fishermen to turn the learned man's world upside down.

With God's amazing grace and after a lot of tension over the whole issue, John's parents did not disown us. It took a little time and prayer, but with God's help I became very close to John's mother over the thirty-three years that I was privileged to know her. When she died at the age of 99, still mentally sharp and full of life, I realized how much she had impacted my life as one of the most influential people I have ever known.

Finding the Afikoman

When John and I became believers in 1975, much of the American church believed in replacement theology; the belief that the Jews were part of an old covenant, and because of their disobedience and unfaithfulness, were cut off from the plan and promises of God. It was also believed that the New Testament church now replaced Israel and received the inheritance of their blessing. As a result, when John and I were born again his Jewish identity faded into the background and we gave ourselves to growing as new believers. I had encountered the person of Jesus in significant ways and was on a quest to intimately know Him. At the same time, we were trying to love and honor John's family and soften the blow of our Christian conversion. We went to synagogue with them on the Jewish High Holidays and celebrated Jewish traditions in their home. At a Passover celebration with John's family during our early days of being Christians, I had my first encounter with the Jewishness of my faith, which came as a total surprise to me.

During the Passover Seder (Seder, meaning order of the evening), I asked a lot of questions because I was trying to understand Judaism. At one point the leader held up a stack of three matzahs (flat squares of unleavened bread), broke the middle one and wrapped it in a white, linen napkin. He then hid it for the children to find later. I asked, "What is that?" He said, "It is called the afikoman, which means, 'the satisfaction'. After the children find it they get a prize and it is the last thing eaten at the end of the meal." I was very interested and asked what the three matzahs symbolized. Their explanation was that they represent their Hebrew patriarchs, Abraham, Isaac, and Jacob. Not satisfied with their answer I asked, "Why is Isaac broken?" They didn't know and I felt their annoyance with my question. This was so confusing to me. This ceremony dates back 3500 years, so how could they have such a weak explanation for what these three matzahs represent? Then the Holy Spirit spoke to me. He said, "It is the Father, Son, and Holy Spirit. The Son is broken, wrapped in a burial cloth and only those with a child-like spirit will find Him. Jesus is the afikoman, the satisfaction."

> *Jesus is the afikoman, the satisfaction*

The impact of His words took me by surprise. When they finally hit my understanding, I was confused and said to Him, "But this is not a Christian ceremony we are doing... What are You doing in this Jewish thing?" I was astounded! I went home that night and asked Jesus, "If Passover is about You then what are the other Jewish festivals about?" He said, "Me, they are all about Me.

10

Christianity is Jewish." I sat there stunned and thought, "No, way!" I suddenly felt that I had struck a gold mine.

My Heart is Marked

This startling revelation that Jesus was Jewish opened a new door of discovery for me. He was inviting me to follow Him on a journey to find the rich treasures about Him and His Kingdom that have been carried and observed by the Jewish people throughout thousands of years of history! Here is the thing that was amazing to me: they faithfully carried what I call, the treasure box of customs, traditions, and the biblical pattern of redemption that the Messiah was to keep. They carried it through overwhelming persecution and almost total annihilation from their enemies. In spite of their often unfaithfulness to God that resulted in His severe discipline to win them back, they persevered. Miraculously, they held on to that "treasure box" for over 3500 years so God could reveal it's mysteries to both Jew and Gentile: His chosen one's for Whom He is coming.

God has done a brilliantly wise thing. At this time in history, when He is moving closer to His second coming to earth, He has purposely set up a divine "stalemate". Paul says, ***"What advantage then has the Jew... Much in every way! Chiefly because to them were committed the oracles of God." (Rom. 3:1-2).*** What have they been given? The "treasure box" of rites, ceremonies, culture and history walking with God through the pattern of redemption for 3500 years, faithfully keeping those "pictures" of Jesus their Messiah alive and yet not knowing that they are all about Him! Just like the ceremony of the

11

afikoman when I first had my eyes opened and He showed me Himself, all the festivals are full of prophetic pictures about Jesus their Messiah.

The Old and New Testaments are full of language about the feasts that Gentile believers do not see, so we miss the full meaning of what is being said. We need to humble ourselves and admit that our Greek understanding will not take us any further without "holding on to the coat of a Jew" and saying, "show us your God". *Zech. 8:23* says,

> *"Thus says the Lord of hosts: 'In those days ten men from every language of the nations shall grasp the sleeve of a Jewish man, saying, "Let us go with you, for we have heard that God is with you."*

Likewise, they have the "treasure box" without any understanding that what they carry only makes sense with the knowledge and revelation of Jesus. I believe when they see us celebrating their festivals in the fullness and joy of knowing Him, they will be moved to jealousy and humbly ask us to show them Jesus. We need them and they need us; what a brilliant idea on God's part so no one can boast! The Jews, as well as the church made up of Jew and Gentile, have been supernaturally blinded until this time in history when He is bringing together "one new man" from the two. This present day merging that has begun will change the face of Christianity and Judaism as we have known them, and will bring, in my opinion, *"life from the dead" (Rom. 11)*.

We are living in a time when God is opening the eyes of the church to understand that we have been adopted into a Jewish family. More than adoption, we are a betrothed people to a Jewish Bridegroom who is coming soon to consummate the ancient Jewish wedding contract that He initiated at His first coming.

So it was, that 38 years ago in 1976, the Holy Spirit took me by the hand and we started our treasure hunt together. I was not seeking to become a scholar; I was seeking to know Him. He was my vision and my reward. He would show me books to read and highlight what He wanted me to see. I took Jewish roots courses, but I felt He wanted me to stop when my head got

> *I felt He wanted me to stop when my head got ahead of my heart*

ahead of my heart and when pride in knowledge made me feel self-righteous for knowing some tidbit of information that others did not have. I had to stay close to His heart and depend completely on the Holy Spirit to lead me and guide me along the way. At first, Judaism seemed difficult to understand and almost mysteriously closed for outsiders to figure out. I did not have a learned rabbi or a Jewish scholar that was able or willing to show me the revelations of Jesus in the feasts. I did not even have the advantage of searching the internet as it did not yet exist. What I did have, however, was the One who taught from **"...Moses and all the Prophets... the things concerning Himself." (Luke 24:27).**

He had me begin as a child by learning from children's books at the library. I would learn how Jews celebrate each feast and then follow their instructions. I began to see them as prophetic pictures in which He wanted to reveal Himself. I would make preparations by setting them up in our home, in churches or rented venues and invite our friends and community to join us. Each year, with each feast, I would ask Him to show me new things and to reveal His heart to me, and my journals are filled with the wonderful things that He showed me about Himself. The joy of finding Him and drawing close to His heart sustained me through the often, lonely journey and reproach for doing that "weird Jewish stuff that was so legalistic"! But God would not let me quit, so year after year we walked through the Jewish calendar and I asked for fresh revelation of Jesus as we did.

Another great resource for learning was taking care of my mother-in-law for all those years; driving her around Denver and being immersed in her world, learning more than what Jewish people believe, but seeing how they live life. I felt the Lord's pleasure in watching another Gentile girl, like Ruth, marry into a Jewish family and cling to her mother-in-law. So it is from the combination of these things, that I want to invite others to begin their own treasure hunt down what I call, **"Ruth's Road", "Finding the Afikoman"** for themselves

As I began my journey of finding Jesus in the feasts, the big picture of what I see today was not yet in focus. We would celebrate the festivals every year and their meaning and revelation unfolded a little more each time we did them, but at the same time, John and I were actively involved in our local church. I did not talk about the "Jewish stuff" very much because at the time, there seemed to be little interest. It was an intimate journey that I hid in my heart and walked out with the Lord.

As John and I grew in our faith and walk with Him, it is hard to pinpoint what things influenced our Christian growth because over the years we were blessed to know and be affected by many quality men and women of God. There were, however, two men who impacted my heart in a significant way. Mike Bickle's teaching on the Song of Solomon (mikebickle.org), the bridal paradigm and his focus on knowing the emotions of God, were life changing for me. The second major influence was being part of our friend, Tim Ruthven's ministry and his teaching on the importance of not just knowing about Jesus, but intimately walking with Him in the Word. He taught us the value of having a heart posture of preparation as a bride waiting for the return of the Bridegroom. The influence of these two men and their revelation of the bridal paradigm became the lens that kept my heart burning and helped me to later connect to the love story hidden in the biblical feasts of the Lord.

It took many years of doing the Jewish holidays and gazing at them with Jesus before I became aware of how prominent the bridal message actually is in the whole Leviticus 23 pattern of the festivals. Over the past 39 years of being a believer I have had two personal encounters with Jesus as my Bridegroom that were about ten years apart. Because of them I am intentionally reading the Word and looking for Him from this point of view. He has been familiar to me as Savior, Father, Judge, Deliverer, Healer and Friend, but the encounters with Him as my Bridegroom have made my heart come alive like no other. So with that in mind, I will share the two bridal encounters that radically changed my relationship with God.

Bridegroom Encounters

In 1981 we went to a church camp in Northern Minnesota called Camp Dominion that was run by Charles and Dottie Schmidt. I thought of myself as an "on fire" charismatic Christian at the time. Unknowingly, I let my earlier innocent and childlike heart grow dull and puffed up with learning the culture of Christianity void of devotionally sitting at His feet. Without even realizing it, I had slowly become distanced from the One that it was all about. Fortunately God's "ways and means" committee intervened on my behalf and He set me up for a fresh revelation of His love.

> *I let my earlier innocent and childlike heart grow dull and puffed up with learning the culture of Christianity void of devotionally sitting at His feet.*

Although the setting of the camp was beautiful, nestled in the middle of a birch forest on a lake, the accommodations were a bit rustic. There was even a sign posted as a joke, warning us that the conditions of the camp were to prepare His end-time army of believers for His return! It is hard to remember what caused me to snap; whether it was the mice running in and out of our room, the bats swooping down near our bed in the night, constant rain and mud getting my new white tennis shoes dirty, the three showers available for 300 people, or the accumulation of everything. But one day, in the outhouse with soggy toilet paper, I started to cry, "God, I hate this place and I do not want to be here with all these people. What is wrong with me that so little feels so hard?" Later I figured out that He was breaking me down so I could realize the barrenness of my heart.

It was in this raw, broken place that I went to hear the afternoon speaker, Art Katz. If you have ever sat under Art's teaching or read his books, you know that he had an intense, prophetic authority from the Lord to speak the truth. His gift, like many Jewish believers I know, was not soft-spoken diplomacy! By the time he got done speaking you could hear a pin drop in the room. To utter even a whisper would have been inappropriate for the heavy

Lord, I know about you... but I do not really know you

conviction of the Holy Spirit that was present. I was undone. I left the meeting, disappeared into the woods, and sat on a rock speechless. Finally the realization hit me and words came out of my mouth; "Lord, I know about you... but I do not really know you. Please help me!"

The next morning I went to a women's gathering in a place set up in the woods called Lydia's tent. A young woman, named Karen Kangas, was sharing her story of tragic loss and grief. Her testimony of Jesus in the midst of it was the catalyst that began my life-changing encounter. Karen shared how in a very short time she lost everything in life that was dear to her. Her house and all her earthly belongings had burnt to the ground in a brush fire, and soon after that her husband was killed in a freak construction accident. She shared her journey of grief that nearly killed her and how Jesus reached out His hand in the midst of her desperation and told her that if she would grab hold of Him He would walk her out of the depression and back into life. After she recounted her daily journey of intimacy with her Bridegroom Jesus, she said an astounding thing; "I am standing here today and can honestly say that even though I lost everything in this world that mattered, what I gained, the treasure of intimately knowing Jesus, is worth much, much more." I was speechless. I saw the countenance of Jesus radiating out of her and I knew it was true. She had found the "Pearl of great price" and I wanted it. I found myself uttering some weighty words in that moment, "Lord, I want to know you... no matter what the cost."

A few hours later, as my husband and I were getting ready to hear our favorite speaker on the last night of the camp, I heard Jesus whisper to my spirit, "Meet me in Lydia's tent at 7 pm." Wow! I was excited and terrified and remembered thinking, "Oh my gosh, God is real and He is actually meeting with me personally." I will always remember the feeling of walking through the Minnesota woods on my way to meet Jesus. I could hear the worship from the distant meeting hall and felt like the chorus they were singing had been orchestrated just for me.

"Lord you are more precious than silver,
Lord you are more costly than gold,
Lord you are more beautiful than diamonds,
and nothing I desire compares to you."

So, with my heart pounding and the beautiful music serenading me, I entered the tent. His presence was there and as I sat in silence before Him, I had heart to heart fellowship with Jesus the Bridegroom for the first time. As we left the next morning, I remember driving away with my heart feeling so lovesick I thought I would die if I could not have more! My heart literally ached to be with Him again all the way home to Colorado.

April 14, 1999

I would love to say that I sailed along on that experience for a long time afterwards. The truth is, it literally changed me forever but the feelings faded, and try as I might, I could not get that wonderful lovesick feeling to return. I asked for it, I sought Him for it, but no matter what I did, I could not manipulate Him to give it to me in my timing. I had other tender encounters with His heart but none could compare to that bridal meeting I had in Lydia's tent in the Minnesota woods. In the 1990's, after renewal broke out in a church in Toronto, I made five trips there and asked for another bridal encounter. I had a great time and got refreshed in the Holy Spirit but He did not answer my prayer until April 14, 1999.

Two friends and I drove to Kansas City to attend a women's conference on intimacy with Jesus, thinking that maybe this was the moment I was waiting for. It was a good conference but my heart felt dead and dull. The last night Diane Bickle did an altar call saying, "Like Snow White asleep under the glass dome, the bride of Christ needs a kiss from Jesus to awaken her heart." She then invited us forward to receive it. Feeling nothing, yet not wanting to miss an opportunity, I went forward and by faith received "the kiss". (Just a note to clarify this statement: Our relationship with Jesus is not to be compared to a human, sexual, relationship. He is not a "boyfriend", so a "kiss" that Diane was praying for was a personal, fresh touch of His presence on our lives to awaken our love for Him which is very scriptural.) Before I left that last night I bought a book that Diane recommended called, Sacred Romance by John Eldridge. Driving back to Colorado I was disappointed again that God was not giving me what I was asking Him for.

Two weeks later I had to keep a dreaded commitment to my mother-in-law. She had just lost her second husband and was feeling lonely. Omi repeatedly asked me if I would go with her to Las Vegas, her favorite vacation spot. The last place on earth that I wanted to go was Las Vegas, but she was so generous to me, and I had built such a close relationship with her that in a weak moment I had agreed. She was in her early nineties at the time, and although she was in amazing shape, she would always take an afternoon nap. I took this opportunity to sit by the pool and read my new book that I had bought at the women's conference two weeks earlier.

We were staying at the Flamingo Hilton and the grounds were beautiful. It was early May and the flowers were blooming, the swans were swimming in the ponds and brides in long, white gowns were having their pictures taken outside the little wedding chapel on the property. To make the romantic picture complete, Frank Sinatra was piped through the speakers singing love songs. Love was in the air! I was feeling drawn by the atmosphere and after a few afternoons of my heart feeling almost cheesy with a feeling of being wooed and in love with love, I had the surprise of my life! I suddenly felt the thick presence of Jesus touching my heart.

I was sitting next to the pool on my lawn chair reading Sacred Romance, and a line in the book said something like, "You have found the love you have always been looking for", and it was as though He jumped out from behind a palm tree! I was undone. Weeping uncontrollably, I had to put my towel over my head to muffle my sobs and to hide my face from curious sunbathers

> *You have found the love you have always been looking for*

around me. I was having my long awaited, much asked for, bridal encounter and I was in "sin city" Las Vegas, Nevada! Not Toronto, not Kansas City, which were much more appropriate places, but in His creative, and totally unpredictable style, He chose to answer me here. By the end of the afternoon I was in the little wedding chapel on

20

my knees, rededicating my life and love to the King of Kings and Creator of the whole universe! Ironically, three days before, I was judging anyone who would come to Las Vegas to get married in a silly, "plastic" wedding chapel, and yet Jesus was not put off by it at all! So with Frank Sinatra crooning love songs through the palm trees, I left Las Vegas love sick again, content that I had received the delayed "kiss" I had asked for two weeks before.

Importance of a Bridal Lens

I continue to seek Him for fresh encounters. I have come to realize that not only is the bridal paradigm a central theme of the entire Bible, it is also the thread that runs through the Jewish festivals. A few years ago it finally occurred to me, "Lord, wait, I finally get it! All these feasts are about a wedding! Is that right?" He said, "Yes, the passion of My heart is to redeem My bride. They are all about a wedding." Wow! It all started to make sense and then I realized that the encounters I had along the way were not disconnected at all, but have served to open my eyes to this reality.

Gary Weins says in his book, <u>Bridal Intercession</u>,

> *"The culmination of human history is a wedding ceremony...* It is this reality that God has held in His heart from the beginning of time. Because this has always been the goal, we can therefore

interpret all of His dealings with human beings in the light of this exhilarating fact."

Gary goes on to say:

"...the bridal analogy is indeed a central theme, (if not the central theme) of God's revelation to us, which provides an interpretive key to understanding His dealings with us... Once we begin to see that is so, and begin to interpret the realities of scripture... the history of Israel, the coming of Christ, His life, His death and resurrection, His dealings with us as we attempt to walk out the life of faith... from the perspective of His heart as the eternal Bridegroom, we begin to understand the unfolding realities of our lives in a completely different way. He has always dealt with us from this perspective. We were created and redeemed for romance." (p.10)

When we look to the end of the story we can see what has been the consuming passion of God's heart from the time man and woman, the crown of His creation, first fell away from Him in the garden. What is the intense focal point... the target-vision... the thing first and foremost on God's heart? What is His purpose in sending Jesus to redeem a people and a planet? Where is this whole thing headed that sums up the point of 6000 years of history?

The answer is found in *Revelation 19:6-9 and 21:2-4:*

"And I heard, as it were, the voice of a great multitude, as the sound of many waters and as the sound of mighty thunderings, saying, "Alleluia! For the Lord God Omnipotent reigns! Let us be glad and rejoice and give Him glory, for the marriage of the Lamb has come, and His wife has made herself ready." And to her it was granted to be arrayed in fine linen, clean and bright, for the fine linen is the righteous acts of the saints. Then he said to me, "Write: 'Blessed are those who are called to the marriage supper of the Lamb!'"

"Then I John, saw the Holy city, New Jerusalem, coming out of heaven from God, prepared as a bride adorned for her husband. And I heard a loud voice from heaven saying, 'Behold, the tabernacle of God is with men, and He will dwell with them, and they shall be His people, God Himself will be with them and be their God. And God will wipe away every tear from their eyes; there shall be no more death, nor sorrow, nor crying. There shall be no more pain, for the former things have passed away."

This is the climax to all of human history... that Day when all things are redeemed and restored and all evil has been removed from the earth, and Jesus reveals His Bride who is perfect and glorious, to all the earth. In a later chapter, I will share with you the traditions of an ancient Jewish wedding that were part of the culture in Jesus' day. But I want to give you one tidbit from that tradition that is important in order to appreciate the fullness of this epic, final scene in the book of Revelation. The word "Apocalypse", conjures up horrific images in our minds of total destruction and chaos. The word in Greek is,"apokalypsis" meaning, "unveiling". A bride in ancient Israel was veiled to the public, but when the bride and groom come out of a wedding chuppah, the bridegroom unveils her for the wedding feast and proudly puts her on display for all to see! I believe that it was from this glorious perspective, that the apostle John was undone watching the grand finale, or closing scene of this age. It was the breathtaking moment of the revelation, or unveiling, of His Bride!!!

I am hoping that as you read this book you will see His unfolding love story from Genesis to Revelation. I pray that you will see that Leviticus 23 is an appointment book of how the Messiah will come to earth to redeem His people, and that it is also the blueprint of our heavenly Father's plan to change our identity from a slave to a son or daughter, then to priests, kings and queens and finally to a bride. It is His story, but it is also yours and it is my pleasure to invite you into it.

*"Abba, Father, hold my affections
and make me a bride prepared for Your Son...
For I know He is worthy of all that I am.
I know the price He's paid and see the great lengths
He has crossed to ask for my hand...
I'm falling in love with Your Son,
the most beautiful man"*

Laura Hackett Park

~ Chapter 2 ~

Tikun Olam

"Do not curse the darkness, kindle the light."
Rabbi Irving Greenberg

After that encounter with Jesus, the Afikoman, at the Passover Seder, I was paying attention to the Jewish world I had married into. There was an underlying theme drawing my heart that was hard to put my finger on. I had never been part of a religion or nationality that had defining characteristics and traditions to call my own. Like many Americans, I was a "Heinz 57" mixture, defined by the culture of the 1950's and 60's that I grew up in. I had always felt a lack of roots, a lack of being able to say I live my life this way because I am Italian or Chinese, or African American or Hispanic. When I became a Christian in 1975 there was a sense of belonging that I had never before experienced, however there was still something missing.

As Christians, our community was centered around meetings. We knew how to meet on Sundays at church or

Wednesdays for small groups, but my question was, "how do we do life?" The main message was to love people, to love God, and to share the good news that Jesus died for our sins so we can live eternally with Him in heaven. That was all important and I was nurturing a personal relationship with Jesus but the reality of our lives at home, behind closed doors, was missing something. Outside of the four hours a week at meetings and trying to be nice people so we could be a good witness for Jesus, we were not given any vision or instructions for what to do in the meantime. I heard a Jewish Rabbi say that the word "Torah" (the first 5 books of the bible) means, "instructions for abundant life". It caught my attention and I was glad that God had left behind an instruction book because I was seeking Him for answers.

> *how do we do life?"*

What I was seeing, being immersed in my mother-in-law's Jewish world and everyday life, was beginning to intrigue me. It was as though they possessed an ingrained understanding and philosophy about life that was consistent. They had more than a common faith, they had a unique worldview, or lens that they viewed life through and abided by. What I observed gave me a desire to grab hold of what it was that was drawing my heart.

One day, while doing an errand for Omi at her synagogue in Denver, it hit me. I went into the gift store and purchased what I needed and then curiously took a tour of the building. In one hallway there was a preschool in session and I saw elderly people from the congregation reading books to the young children. I noticed a picture hanging on the wall called, "generation to generation", depicting the concept of passing the baton to those that come after you… being responsible for them and allowing

28

them to, "stand on your shoulders." There was a sense of a common destination they were heading towards, and they needed to help each other get there. Everywhere I went in the building I felt life and community. No one goes through life alone. Old people are cared for and single people are part of families. It's not possible to stay single long though; there is a city full of people in the Jewish community that all know each other and are committed to make matches for their sons and grandsons. Once the match is made they are all invited to the wedding, where they know how to rejoice and celebrate together. Sometime in the future, at the circumcision of the new baby, the community gathers again to celebrate with choruses of, "L'Chaim", "To life"! When someone dies, they faithfully come every day for seven days bringing meals and praying for the one in mourning. They are more than community; they are a family, knit together with a common thread that goes back thousands of years.

I went into the women's restroom and broke down crying. I was jealous. What was I jealous of? They are part of something bigger than themselves, and like generations before them, they are held together with a glue that was not based on agreement over doctrines of their faith; it is much deeper and binding than that. Whether conservative or reformed, orthodox or Hasidic, they are a unified people who know who they are,

> *they are a unified people who know who they are, know how to live*

know how to live, and have a vision of where they are going. They are contrary and separate from the world yet, at the same time, can fully participate in its redemption. I wanted to be part of them and I wanted to do life like they did but there was one thing standing in my way; I loved

Jesus and He was not welcome here, which meant I was not welcome here either.

I made a decision in the women's restroom that day. I told God that I was really jealous for what the Jewish people had and that I was confused because the New Testament says that the church is supposed to make them jealous! Clearly something was wrong, but I made my choice and told Jesus I would rather have Him... but if there was a way to have Him and these things, that would be wonderful. I left the synagogue knowing that if I never found the life I had experienced and longed for that day... He was enough. The person of Jesus was a non-negotiable. He was the center of my world and I was not willing to go anywhere without Him. But I was still conflicted about the jealousy I had experienced and it prompted me to nag Him until He gave me some answers. What is the mysterious vision and sense of destiny that the Jewish people carry in their souls? I had to know. God used Rabbi Irving Greenberg to answer my question.

> *What is the mysterious vision and sense of destiny that the Jewish people carry in their souls?*

Jewish Mandate of Redemption

In his book, <u>The Jewish Way</u>, Rabbi Greenberg says, "The central paradigm of Jewish religion is redemption." He then says that because human beings are made in the image of God, each person is unique and has equal, infinite value. The majority of people throughout history have lived undignified lives under poverty and oppression, and

Judaism affirms that this will one day be overcome and paradise will be restored to the earth. Greenberg says,

> **"The Jewish religion is founded on the divine assurance and human belief that the world will be perfected. Life will triumph over its enemies: war, oppression, hunger, poverty, sickness and even death. Before we are done, humanity will achieve the fullest realization of the dignity of the human being. In the messianic era, the earth will become a paradise and every human being will be recognized and treated as an image of God. In a world of justice and peace, with all material needs taken care of, humans will be free to establish a harmonious relationship with nature, with each other, with God." (p.18)**

Rabbi Greenberg then explains that their goal and vision of restoring the world to the Garden of Eden needs a way to be walked out and sustained through history. It had to be consistently valued and passed on to future generations so the dream of redemption could be kept alive. How is this achieved? Rabbi Greenberg answers this question:

> **"Through the Jewish way of life and the holidays, the Torah seeks to nurture the infinite love and unending faith needed to sustain people until perfection is achieved... According to classic Judaism, God alone is the divine ground of life but**

God has chosen a partner in the perfection process. The ultimate goal will be achieved through human participation." (pp. 18-19)

At the foundation of the Jewish way of life is the belief that God has covenanted with mankind to restore paradise to the earth; to once again have a place to dwell in close relationship with men and women, with all evil and darkness removed. His plan of redemption was set in motion first with Noah in covenant with all mankind. Then later, He chose one man, Abraham, and made a covenant with him that, *"I will make you a great nation... And in you all the families of the earth shall be blessed." (Gen. 12: 2-3)*.

The pivotal event for the Jewish people, and the whole earth, was the Exodus out of Egypt; where God took a multitude of slaves and brought them to a mountain to enter into a marriage covenant (Ex. 19). It was on Mt. Sinai where as a kingdom of priests... His betrothed... a holy nation, were given the mandate to partner with Him to redeem the world so His throne could one day come down to earth. They believe that every Jew, past, present and future, was on Mt. Sinai and entered into this covenant relationship to perfect the fallen world with Him.

One of the best sermons I have ever heard was preached by a Rabbi at synagogue on the festival of Shavuot (Pentecost). He was reminding the people that each one of them was at Mt. Sinai 3500 years ago and said yes to the call to redeem the world. Passion for his message gripped him as he told them who they were and how they were failing to live their lives according to this privileged assignment they were given. It was solemn and sobering in the room because of the quiet conviction that settled like a thick cloud. The Rabbi lay prostrate on the ground crying as the congregation filed out. At a later date I made a very "Gentile" move that I regretted. I asked if he had a recording of that Shavuot message so I could hear it again. He looked at me in disbelief and said, "Recording? We do not record here. That message was alive for that moment in time."

> *"Recording? We do not record here. That message was alive for that moment in time."*

This vision and goal of redemption is the main theme and philosophy that runs through all of Jewish life. In the famous Sermon on the Mount in Matthew 5-7, Jesus is reminding the Jews present that day of their calling and mandate, and how they are to live carrying the torch of redemption. He says,

> *"You are the salt of the earth; but if the salt loses its flavor, how shall it be seasoned? It is then good for nothing but to be thrown out and trampled underfoot by men. You are the light of the world. A city that is set on a hill cannot be hidden. Nor do they light a lamp and put it under a basket, but on a lamp stand, and it gives light to all who are in the house. Let your light so shine before men, that they may see your good works and glorify your Father in heaven."*
>
> ***Matt. 5:13-16***

Lesson of Tikun Olam at a Jewish Funeral

I saw this philosophy of redemption woven through much of Jewish life. It is called "tikun olam", meaning, "repairing the world". Life always triumphs over death; light always removes darkness, everything and everyone broken and bound will be healed and set free. If a funeral procession and a wedding procession meet at an intersection, the wedding passes first because life has precedence over death. If tragedy strikes, you do not become a victim, you rise up and rebuild or redeem. If evil manifests itself, "You do not curse the darkness, you kindle a light" (Greenberg, The Jewish Way, p.156).

I got to observe this walked out in life when I attended my first Jewish funeral at the death of John's father. The service was graveside and the mourners were gathered there. Six Jewish men carried the simple pine casket with the Star of David carved on top. Everyone began to cry, some people wailed. The man next to me was a close friend and boarder in my in-law's home. He was sobbing, so I did another "unkosher" move; I reached out and patted him on the arm to console him. You do not do that! The Bible says in *Ecclesiastes 3:4*, that there is a time for everything; *"A time to weep, and a time to laugh; A time to mourn, and a time to dance..."* This was a time to mourn. You allow emotions for a time. If you don't, you shove them down inside which is unhealthy. I automatically tried to comfort because I was uncomfortable with the outward show of emotions that I was never taught to value. I offended the man by comforting him before mourning had passed and he pushed my arm off his sleeve and said, "Please don't do that".

After my father-in-law's life was honored, and scriptures proclaiming God's goodness were read, some dirt from Israel was put on the coffin, and then one by one, friends and family walked by and put a shovel full of dirt in the grave. They were together in life, and now they were part of each other in death. The family mourns at home for seven days with friends tending to their meals and needs, and praying with them daily. Then, on the seventh day, the mourner, (in this case, John's mother), gets up, washes her face, gets dressed, walks around the block and chooses life. The mourning time is over and while grieving is still there, you make a proclamation choosing to live again. Life always wins! If you do not make an intentional choice to go on living, depression takes over and death not only gets the one you lost, but gets you as well. Jews have a mandate to live, to rebuild, and to not ever let the enemy win, so that generations behind you can choose life also.

> *Jews have a mandate to live, to rebuild, and to not ever let the enemy win*

Choosing to Live as Redeemers Every Day

Our life is not our own. We do not get the luxury of quitting. We keep living for those who are in our lives and for those who come after. We are a community of redeemers. God left instructions on how to live. We keep going, we keep living, and we keep proclaiming the vision that in the end we win!!! In order to get to the end goal of paradise restored and God ruling as King over the whole earth, every generation has to "play by the rules" and live as redeemers in order to carry the torch for the next generation. We are to live our lives in a way that when we die, the world and people we touched are in better shape than we found them.

Jesus was the perfect example of living "tikun olam". The book of Acts says,

> *"The word which God sent to the children of Israel, preaching peace through Jesus Christ— He is Lord of all— that word you know, which was proclaimed throughout all Judea, and began from Galilee after the baptism which John preached: how God anointed Jesus of Nazareth with the Holy Spirit and with power, who went about doing good and healing all who were oppressed by the devil, for God was with Him."*
>
> *Acts 10:36-38*

Again in *Matthew 9:35,*

> *"Then Jesus went about all the cities and villages, teaching in their synagogues, preaching the gospel of the kingdom, and healing every sickness and every disease among the people."*

We need to partner with Jesus every day and ask Him, "Who are we going to bring redemption to today? Who are we going to encourage? Give me opportunities to 'go about doing good'." Some days He will have us do big things, but even a smile that tells someone that you value them can be healing to a heavy heart. We are partners with Him and we have an assignment to bring salt and light and life wherever we go. Then when we come together we can be excited and encourage each other with the testimonies of how a living God touched hearts and we had the privilege of partnering with Him in the process. Too often the body of Christ is bound together by having the same doctrines and agreeing on the same issues, but sadly once there is disagreement, our ties with each other are broken. Jews have a strong bond because as a people they have the same prophetic history… the same enemies that hate them wherever they go… the same assignment given to them on Mt. Sinai… and a marriage covenant they said yes to together, which can be ignored but never severed. They accepted the responsibility to choose life and to bring life wherever they can. They are part of a continuum, marching towards a day when Paradise is restored, and each person's life is an opportunity to add a small part in the process until the vision of final redemption is achieved. It is this Jewish mandate of "repairing the world" that we are grafted into. This is our inheritance as believers in a Jewish Messiah.

> *Jews have a strong bond because as a people they have the same prophetic history…*

"Now to Abraham and his Seed were the promises made. He does not say, "And to seeds," as of many, but as of one, "And to your Seed," who is Christ... And if you are Christ's, then you are Abraham's seed, and heirs according to the promise."

Gal. 3:16, 29

Longing for the Final Redemption

Being part of this bigger plan of redemption excites me. Before I discovered my Hebrew roots I felt dissatisfied with my narrow view of heaven and what we were living for. I was thankful for what Jesus did for me by coming to earth and dying for my sins so that I could spend eternity with Him, but I longed for something more that I did not yet understand. I had no vision for the present and no real vision for eternity beyond how it benefited me. I was longing for something to be part of that was bigger than myself. When my heart began to connect to the love story in the Jewish festivals I got a glimpse of the real reward in this whole gospel story. It is not first and foremost about us and what we get. It is about Him and what He has longed for and anguished over and grieved for over the last 6,000 years! He lost a bride and He lost the place that He prepared to dwell with her. We get the honor and the privilege of partnering with Him to restore and heal mankind and repair the world with Him so the Father's throne can come to earth! We are His portion, His treasure, His inheritance. The reward of His suffering is one day in the future, seeing His bride adorned and made perfect for her Husband, coming down from heaven (Rev 19, 21)! I believe that deep in our spirits we all long for more than heaven, and scripture testifies that this is true.

> *We get the honor and the privilege of partnering with Him to restore and heal mankind and repair the world with Him so the Father's throne can come to earth!*

"For the earnest expectation of the creation eagerly waits for the revealing of the sons of God. For the creation was subjected to futility, not willingly, but because of Him who subjected it in hope; because the creation itself also will be delivered from the bondage of corruption into the glorious liberty of the children of God. For we know that the whole creation groans and labors with birth pangs together until now. Not only that, but we also who have the firstfruits of the Spirit, even we ourselves groan within ourselves, eagerly waiting for the adoption, the redemption of our body."

Rom. 8:19-23

Deep in our souls there is a longing for God to come and make all things right. We long for all injustice, evil, and suffering to be vindicated and removed, and for goodness, safety and peace to rule. We all love endings where the good guy wins and everyone lives happily ever after. We long for it because God longs for it and from the moment He lost all in the Garden of Eden, He initiated a plan of how He was going to get everything back. The blueprint of this plan of redemption is found in the Leviticus 23 biblical feasts. He gave the festivals to His people to keep their dream and vision for final redemption alive so that through a history of constant oppression, they would believe in it, and wait for it, and not lose heart.

Rabbi Greenberg says this:

"By some astonishing divine grace and by the peculiar experiences of their history, a people... the Jews... have become a key vehicle for the realization of a perfect world... How to inspire a people with the vision of final perfection? How to supply the strength to persevere for millennia on the road to redemption with out selling out?... The key is found in the 'halalcha', the Jewish way of life, and it's primary pedagogical tools; the Jewish calendar and the Jewish holidays."

<u>The Jewish Way</u>, p. 20

Goel / Redeemer

The Jewish people have always understood that this final redemption would be realized with a messianic figure, or an "anointed one" to come. He would be their "goel", or redeemer, to pay a price for their redemption. **(See Appendix G)** Every tribe in ancient Israel had a "goel". If misfortune struck or if a tribe member inadvertently committed a crime and was held captive by another, the "goel" would pay a price, or buy back, so the person could be redeemed and go free. We see an example of this in the book of Ruth when Boaz becomes a redeemer, a goel, for Naomi's inheritance by marrying Ruth and preserving her lineage. The future coming of the goel for the nation and the whole earth has been proclaimed as a prayer for thousands of years. It says, **"I believe with perfect faith in the coming of the mashiach (messiah), and though he may tarry, still I await him every day"** (Ani Ma'amin, from Rambam's 13 principles of the faith).

This excerpt explains it further:

> **"Belief in the eventual coming of the mashiach is a basic and fundamental part of traditional Judaism... In the Shemoneh Esrei prayer, recited three times daily, we pray for all of the elements of the coming of the mashiach: ingathering of the exiles; restoration of the religious courts of justice; an end of wickedness, sin and heresy; reward to the righteous; rebuilding of Jerusalem; restoration of the line of King David; and restoration of Temple service."**
> Judaism 101, the messiah, www.jewfaq.org

Jews throughout history did not understand that the coming messiah would come as God in the flesh; this idea was not fathomable to them. The incarnation is unfathomable to us as Christians and yet we know it is true. How can we begin to wrap our minds around the idea of God loving His bride so much that He would send His Son in the likeness of sinful flesh to become one with us? They saw him to be a chosen, anointed, highly charismatic leader and deliverer like Moses. In *Deuteronomy 18:18 God says to Moses,*

*"I will raise up for them a Prophet like
you from among their brethren, and will
put My words in His mouth, and He shall
speak to them all that I command Him."*

Two Concepts of Messiah

The Jewish people have always seen two different
concepts in scripture about the messiah. Because they
studied, read through the scriptures every year, and read
weekly portions every Sabbath, they were very familiar with
the prophecies about his future coming. They saw the one
whom they called "suffering servant" or messiah ben
Joseph who was also known as "son of man". The
scriptures portraying Him this way are the following: Dan.
9:26; Zech. 9:9; Zech. 12:10; Is. 40-53, (see especially, Is.
52:13-15 and Is. 53:2-9); Ps. 22. They also saw the
"conquering King" known as messiah ben David. Some
examples of this concept are found in the following verses:
Is. 63-66; Jer. 23:5-6; Zech. 14:1-4,9; Ps. 2:6-8. At the time
of Jesus in the first century, there was a heightened
expectation of the coming messiah. At the very core of
Judaism was the belief that when this "anointed one" came,
He would establish God's kingdom on earth and their
oppression from ungodly empires would be ended. They
had read the scriptures about the suffering servant but had
a hard time grasping His significance in the midst of world
events around them. The history of the Jews is one of
persecution and oppression, so their main focus by the
time of Jesus was looking for the conquering King Messiah
that would deal with their enemies, set up His kingdom,
and rule in Jerusalem. When Jewish theologians looked at

the two concepts of Messiah found in scripture, they were
conflicted. One was despised, persecuted, lowly and
humiliated, while the other was powerful, anointed to crush
the enemy and usher in the golden messianic age in Israel.
They did not know how to reconcile these completely
opposite messianic figures. The following excerpt from the
Midrash (a Jewish commentary on the Torah), had this to
say about the two concepts of the messiah:

> "And when the days of the Messiah
> arrive, <u>Gog and Magog</u> will come up
> against the Lord of Israel, because they
> will hear that Israel is without a king and
> sits in safety. Instantly they will take with
> them seventy-one nations and go up to
> Jerusalem, and they will say; "Pharaoh
> was a fool to command that the males [of
> the Israelites] be killed and to let the
> females live. Balaam was an idiot that he
> wanted to curse them and did not know
> that their God had blessed them. Haman
> was insane in that he wanted to kill them,
> and he did not know their God can save
> them. I shall not do as they did, but shall
> fight against their God first, and thereafter
> I shall slay them…" And the Holy One,
> blessed be He, will say to him; "You
> wicked one! You want to wage war against
> Me? By your life, I shall wage war against
> you! Instantly the Holy One, blessed be
> He will cause hailstones, which are
> hidden in the firmament, to descend upon
> him, and will bring upon him a great

plague... And after him will arise another king, wicked and insolent, and he will wage war against Israel for three months, and his name is <u>Armilus</u>. And these are his marks; he will be bald, one of his eyes will be small, the other big. His right arm will be only as long as a hand... And he will go up to Jerusalem and will slay <u>Messiah ben Joseph</u>... And thereafter will come <u>Messiah ben David</u>... And he will kill the wicked Armilus... And thereafter the Holy One, blessed be He, will gather all Israel who are dispersed here and there."

Midrash Vayosha 19

From this quote we can see their conclusion that two different messianic figures would come, which further explains John the Baptist's question to Jesus when he was in prison under Herod: *"...Are You the Coming One, or do we look for another?" (Luke 7:19).* John the Baptist did not doubt that Jesus was the Messiah, he was just asking, "which one are you? Are you suffering servant or conquering king? Or, are you going to fulfill all of the scriptures about both at this time?" John wanted Jesus to tell him if He was at this time coming to take over, or if he was going to possibly die at the hands of Herod. He had a valid personal reason to want an explanation of what the plan was!

> *John the Baptist did not doubt that Jesus was the Messiah*

Many of the Jews in Jesus' day missed the time of His visitation. They had become more focused on the politics concerning Israel and getting free from Roman rule, not realizing that the true freedom that Jesus brought at His first coming was healing to dead hearts as they saw the love of the Father demonstrated in His Son. Even His disciples who knew He was the Messiah were blind to the suffering servant and were confused and despairing when He was left defeated on the cross. Jesus addressed this confusion when the two men on the road to Emmaus expressed their disappointment because they had put all their hope in the certainty of a doctrine that perceived Jesus to be their conquering King. Jesus said to them,

> *"...O foolish ones, and slow of heart to believe in all that the prophets have spoken! Ought not the Christ to have suffered these things and to enter into His glory?"*
>
> *Luke 24:25-26*

Also in Acts it says,

> *"But those things which God foretold by the mouth of all His prophets, that the Christ would suffer, He has thus fulfilled"*
>
> *Acts 3:18*

As New Testament believers we are in danger of making the same mistake in missing His appointments. We clearly see the suffering servant Messiah that Jesus fulfilled at His first coming. The problem is if we leave Him on the cross eternally we fail to see that the next time He comes down to earth His mission of redemption will look totally different. When a king of Israel rode into Jerusalem riding

45

on a donkey he was announcing peace; when he rode in on a white horse, he was announcing war. We have seen the suffering servant, King Jesus fulfilled by this scripture:

> *"Rejoice greatly, O daughter of Zion! Shout, O daughter of Jerusalem! Behold, your King is coming to you; He is just and having salvation, Lowly and riding on a donkey, A colt, the foal of a donkey."*
>
> *Zech. 9:9*

We have yet to see the conquering King Jesus Who will come again to fulfill the scripture in *Revelation 19:11:*

> *"Now I saw heaven opened, and behold, a white horse. And He who sat on him was called Faithful and True, and in righteousness He judges and makes war. His eyes were like a flame of fire, and on His head were many crowns. He had a name written that no one knew except Himself. He was clothed with a robe dipped in blood, and His name is called The Word of God."*

People always ask, "Why have most Jews missed seeing Jesus as their Messiah?" Because they had the wrong perception of the One they were looking for. A mangled, defeated man, humiliated and dying on a Roman cross was not the King of their theological expectations. They were looking for the Revelations 19 King on a white horse with the fire of justice and vindication in His eyes, announcing war with His enemies. As a result, they missed "the time of their visitation". As born again believers, we embrace the Messiah that they disdained; but is it possible when the Jews are welcoming the Revelation 19 Messiah that they have always been looking for, that we will miss the time of His second visitation because we are offended by the Man with His robes stained in blood? Just a sobering thought to consider.

Two Agricultural Seasons

Another clue God left behind for us to see these two comings of the future Messiah was in the two agricultural seasons in the land of Israel. God tells Moses in Leviticus 23 that He has seven festivals throughout the year that He wants to celebrate with His people. The first four occur in the spring harvest time, known in Israel as the former rain. They are:

- **Passover**
- **Feast of Unleavened Bread**
- **Festival of First Fruits of the Barley Harvest**
- **Feast of Weeks known as Shavuot**

These are the feasts that the suffering servant, Jesus, fulfilled at His first coming to earth. The main crops harvested are, first barley and then wheat. When you see these crops mentioned in the Bible, they are clues that point to specific things that happen in that spring season! It is very significant that Ruth came with Naomi to Bethlehem Judah at the barley harvest! I will explain why in a later chapter... I just want to draw your attention to the fact that even the crops mentioned in a verse are pointing to something important.

The last three festivals occur in the fall harvest time, known as the latter rain. They are:

- **Feast of Trumpets**
- **Yom Kippur "Day of Atonement"**
- **Feast of Tabernacles**

To see a chart of both the spring and fall feasts take a look at **Appendix B and C.**

The crops associated in this season are mainly fruits, olives, and grapes. You will begin to notice many scriptures mentioning the grape harvest and many times it is a reference to specific things that God is going to do during that fall harvest time that speaks of His second coming as conquering King. There is a very interesting verse in *Hosea 6:3* that is another clue to reveal the mystery of when the Messiah will come:

> *"Let us know, Let us pursue the knowledge of the LORD. His going forth is established as the morning; He will come to us like the rain, Like the latter and former rain to the earth."*

Did you catch that? The Messiah will come during the former rain in the spring and the latter rain in the fall! Two manifestations that He will fulfill when He comes… are Suffering Servant and Conquering King… First the Suffering Servant will come in the spring harvest, then He will come again as Conquering King during the fall harvest… and water (bring life to) the earth. But the clues to His coming and the details of what He will do when He comes, get even more specific. Jesus has an appointment book and His appointments that He promised to keep are written on the Hebrew, lunar calendar. I want you to see it with your own eyes so please open to Leviticus 23. It is the chapter in the

> *It is the chapter in the Bible that holds the divine blueprint of our whole redemption story*

Bible that holds the divine blueprint of our whole redemption story… for Israel, for the church, and for the whole world.

A Close Look at Leviticus 23:2

As you read the following verses, I want you to take notice of some important words and phrases. First, I want you to underline in your bible that the last words in verse 2 says, "These are My feasts". He does not say they are Jewish feasts, although the Jewish people have faithfully kept them for thousands of years. They are God's feasts. That means they are our feasts!

The next thing I want you to underline is the word "feasts" mentioned two times in this verse. The word in Hebrew is "moed" and it means "appointment" or "appointed time". *Lev. 23:1-2 reads:*

> *"And the LORD spoke to Moses, saying, "Speak to the children of Israel, and say to them: 'The feasts of the LORD, which you shall proclaim to be holy convocations, these are My feasts."*

Now look at **Genesis 1:14,**

"Then God said, "Let there be lights in the firmament of the heavens to divide the day from the night; and let them be for signs and seasons, and for days and years;"

The word "seasons" in this verse is the same Hebrew word for "feasts" in Leviticus 23! It is "moed," or "appointment"! The Hebrew word for "signs" is "owth", meaning, "signal". So what Genesis 1:14 is actually saying is very interesting. It is saying that the moon and the sun were made to signal His appointed times that He would come to the earth!

the moon and the sun were made to signal His appointed times that He would come to the earth!

God is saying in Leviticus 23:2 that He has appointments on an appointment calendar and those appointments are portrayed in His feasts! Let's look at the next interesting word in Leviticus 23:2, "holy convocation". It is the Hebrew word "miqrah", meaning "rehearsal" or "dress rehearsal". So what God is telling His people is that the festivals listed in Leviticus 23 are on His appointment book that He is going to keep, and He wants them to not just know what they are; He wants them to do them, observe them or rehearse them like a dress rehearsal before the big production so that when it is time for the real live event in the future… when He actually comes to fulfill it on the earth… WE WILL NOT MISS IT!

Hebrew learning is with the senses. When a Jewish child begins to study the Torah, the teacher will put honey on his or her tongue to remind them that God's word is sweet. In *1 John 1:1, it says,*

"That which was from the beginning, which we have heard, which we have seen with our eyes, which we have looked upon, and our hands have handled, concerning the Word of life--".

Greek learning is mostly cerebral. It is learning concepts through reasoning to form logical conclusions. Hebrew thinking and learning involves the senses and emotions as well as their minds. Biblical Jews did not merely think about truth, they experienced it. They walked in truth by living it rather than talking

> *They walked in truth by living it rather than talking about it and analyzing it.*

about it and analyzing it. God wants us to do more than learn facts about the feasts; rather He wants us to do and experience them to remind our hearts of Who He is. (For a rich study on understanding Hebrew thought, I recommend Marvin Wilson's book, Our Father Abraham.)

Another Hebrew word to consider in your word study is "quarah" which in English means, "to proclaim". *Leviticus 23:4 reads,*

"These are the feasts of the LORD, holy convocations which you shall proclaim at their appointed times."

The word "proclaim" in this verse means to actually stop them and bid them to come, or to invite. This is echoed in *Matthew 22:3-4 when Jesus:*

> *"...sent out his servants to call those who were invited to the wedding; and they were not willing to come."*

God is inviting His people to come celebrate His festivals that are His appointments on His appointment calendar. He wants us to rehearse them and experience them as a community going somewhere together... because they are all a picture of Him, and clues to how He is coming to earth to reclaim His people and the place He chose to dwell.

These spring feasts were formalized in Leviticus 23 and the children of Israel were to keep them forever to remember what God had done for them and what He was going to do in the future. The astounding reality that we absolutely have to stop and take notice of is this: the pattern that they were rehearsing year after year to commemorate their dramatic rescue out of Egypt that is recorded in Exodus 12 through 19, was repeated perfectly when Jesus came down to earth!!! As we rehearse this story together in Chapter 5, we will see His divine romance hidden in the gospels where the unfolding plan of a heavenly Bridegroom and King came to redeem, or buy back, His bride. I want to show you how Jesus followed the pattern of an ancient Jewish wedding, paid for His bride with His own blood, left her the gift of the Holy Spirit and right now is preparing a place to take her when He comes again as conquering King. He will vindicate her with His righteous justice as He deals with all His enemies and restores the earth to paradise once more!

For the next book, ***Watching and Waiting: Discovering Jesus in the Fall Feasts***, we will look at the pattern of the fall feasts that is found in Leviticus 23 and is also walked out by Moses in the book of Exodus from chapters 19-40. It is a glorious glimpse of what Jesus will fulfill at His second coming! We have to view it like an epic screenplay and if all we see is half the movie of His first coming as suffering servant Messiah, we miss the grand finale of Him getting the reward of His suffering! Jesus paid a price for His bride (all those who believe in Him) and left instructions for us to watch and wait for Him to return because one day there is going to be a wedding!! There is a Day coming that is for His heart to rejoice and be glad. He saw this Day in the future, before He died, and it was ***"… for the joy that was set before Him endured the cross …" (Heb. 12:2).***

In the last book of the Bible, a lovesick bride is yearning for Him to come, and a magnificent King arrayed in wedding garments comes down to answer the call! (See Rev. 22:17) The Jews are looking for a King to fight and win a final war for them and vindicate them from their enemies so they can rule the earth by His side. As a Christian I used to be satisfied with a savior that died for my sins so I could live with Him in heaven forever. Both of these are good but they fall way short of the glory of the story that He had in His heart from the beginning of time. He is the One Who is the center of this story. It is His heart that has been scorned, forsaken, betrayed, slandered and crushed for 6,000 years. It is when we lay down our self-focus of what-is-in-it-for-us and connect with His emotions that will cause our hearts to burn until He gets what He has always wanted and what He justly deserves. He becomes a suffering servant to make His bride perfect and compatible in holiness. He becomes a conquering King to vindicate her heart and His, rid the earth of evil and once again have a perfect place to dwell with the ones He loves. Not on heaven... on earth!!!

God is partnering with His covenant bride to bring tikun olam. He sent the Goel / Redeemer to accomplish this plan. He will send Him again to finish it! The way to walk in this vision and reality is to proclaim and rehearse it, to personally encounter this reality weekly and yearly as we walk with Him on His calendar and celebrate His feasts with Him. How do we do that? One step at a time. I could not begin this journey myself until my heart was convinced. I was on a search to know Him, and if learning the Jewish roots of my faith had been a distraction to that end, I would not have continued just to find interesting knowledge alone. I kept showing up because He did too! So my challenge in writing this book is to share with you my revelations, testimonies, and encounters along with some gleanings of foundational teaching with the goal of leaving your hearts strengthened in the knowledge of His love for you and burning with unquenchable love-sickness for Him. Encountering Him in His feasts is one of the trails for you to get there.

Rabbi Greenberg says,

> **"Judaism is the Jewish way to get humanity from the world as it is now, to the world of final perfection. To get from**

here to there, you need both the goal and a process to keep you going over the long haul of history. In Judaism, the holidays supply both."

The Jewish Way, p. 24

I invite you to fall in love with Leviticus 23 as He "bids you to come", so He can take you on a journey of revelation and encounter that leads to a bridal chamber! This is not a fairy tale. It is real, and it really does end in living "happily ever after".

"For your Maker is your husband,
The LORD of hosts is His name;
And your Redeemer (Goel) is the Holy One of Israel;
He is called the God of the whole earth."

Is. 54:6 (parenthesis mine)

~ Chapter 3 ~

The Rock From Which You Were Hewn
Is. 51:1

"And if you are Christ's, then you are Abraham's seed, and heirs according to the promise"
Gal. 3:29

I believe we are living at a time in church history when God wants to reveal to us our rich inheritance that Paul alludes to in **Romans 11:17**. Paul tells the Gentile believers that they are, **"...grafted in among them, and with them became a partaker of the root and fatness of the olive tree"**. I read this verse for years but without really asking myself the question, what does Paul mean that Gentiles are "grafted in"? When recently sharing at a small group, I asked them this same question, curious to know what their answers would be. Most, like me, had never really thought about it with any kind of depth. There was a general agreement among the group that they understood Paul was saying we were connected to a Jewish root but what that really meant was undefined for them. We talked some about what our impressions of Judaism were in general, and I realized that for the majority of Christians, Judaism is a mysterious religion with rituals that seem tedious and antiquated. We automatically sum up their beliefs in the emphatic statement, "The Jews are under the law and we are under grace". It has been a neat and tidy way to dismiss their relevance and to distance ourselves from their "legalistic view" of God and life. But that conclusion presents us with a problem. Paul says we have been grafted into their tree and have now become one with them because of Jesus. Also, their root and all that it contains now supports us and gives us life! So, if that is true, and

> *why in the world would He graft us into a dead, old, lifeless tree???*

Jesus came to give us abundant life and set us free, why in the world would He graft us into a dead, old, lifeless tree???

As Christians, we have an irrational phobia that as soon as you mention anything Jewish, you are going to shackle us to some weird list of laws and make us wear skull caps and blow shofars! I understand that some expressions of messianic Judaism have carried an imposing, religious spirit, but we should not throw the baby out with the bathwater! We have to believe that there is something vital and nurturing and life giving at that ancient root that the enemy has stolen and "twisted", like he does, to keep us from wanting to enter into that grafted in identity. Romans 11 is a roadblock. It is staring us in the face and it should not be minimized or ignored any longer. I understand the resistance. I understand that it is all very "messy" and easier to keep tip-toeing around the issue of how this whole Jew and Gentile identity crisis can possibly be resolved... but it is time to deal with it and I am hoping my story will help you navigate through this quagmire of issues and misunderstanding. I will break the weightiness of my last paragraph with a funny story about an experience at my first Jewish ceremony… our son's circumcision.

My First Jewish Ceremony

Our son, Benjamin was born in 1976. We were new Christians and in the midst of intense strife with John's parents as a result of our conversion. My mother-in-law, Omi, had one mission on her mind; she would not sleep at night until I became a Jew. She was only 4ft. 6 inches, but she was a force to be reckoned with! She had looked the Nazi prison guards in the face and demanded they let her husband out of jail for the day and they listened! She was not giving up but I was not giving in. My one concession was to agree to honor them by taking part in their holidays and traditions.

After Ben was born, the issue of circumcision came up and John's parents asked if we would respect their wishes and do a Jewish bris (circumcision). I thought, what would it hurt, we wanted it done anyway, and what would it matter if it was on the first day or the eighth day after birth, so we agreed. Oh my goodness! If I had only known what we were saying yes to, I would never have gone along with it! A group of men from the Jewish community came to our house. Then a man with a scraggly beard in a dark suit came to the door carrying a bag full of "instruments". He was the one to perform the circumcision. I asked Omi, "Is he the doctor?" She said, no, he was the mohel. "Where is the doctor", I asked. She said we did not need a doctor, because the mohel does the surgery. What? Then the men and the "mohel", went into our son's bedroom and started praying and chanting some prayers in Hebrew. What happened next put me in a panic. They tied him to this rustic board that looked like it had survived the dark ages! This was primitive and barbaric. Where was the clean, sterile procedure room at the hospital with white drapes and real doctors with rubber gloves??? I left the room when "the instrument", used in the time of Abraham for sure, came out of the black bag! I ran to the backyard and broke down crying.

I later learned the spiritual meaning of that ceremony and was deeply touched by it. It is taken from **Leviticus 12:3: "And on the eighth day the flesh of his foreskin shall be circumcised."** It is interesting that on the eighth day there is more vitamin K in your body than at any other time in your life. This is the blood-clotting vitamin, so even on a practical level, the eighth day was a logical time for a surgical procedure. The baby is carried into the place where the circumcision is performed; usually in the synagogue but sometimes the home. In ancient times it was done in the temple. Then the mother gives the baby to two "messengers", usually a man and a woman, who bless him and carry him to the "sandek". A sandek is a righteous man, usually a grandfather or an important male figure in a family. The sandek takes a priestly role and sits in what is known as "Elijah's chair". His job is to hold the baby still for the circumcision. When the mohel sees the baby coming, he declares, "baruch ha ba", "blessed is he who comes". After the circumcision is complete, the men who are present as witnesses pray the following: that the baby will keep his covenant relationship with God, that he will study the Torah so he can have life; that he will one day come to the wedding canopy; and that he will be a righteous man doing good deeds bringing redemption.

Then the baby's name is proclaimed, a blessing is said over wine, and a few drops of wine are placed on the baby's tongue.

I wondered if this ancient ceremony is what took place in Luke 2:21-38, when Mary and Joseph brought Jesus to the temple to be circumcised. Were Simeon and Anna the "messengers" in the ceremony that blessed Him and presented Him for circumcision? I am remembering my initial reaction as a new mom watching my infant son go through this ancient ritual and judging it as primitive and barbaric, not understanding what it was all about. I am not saying that all parents should go through a Jewish bris with their sons. That is not my point. But what I am pointing out is, what to us is just a quick medical procedure in a hospital, can actually be a meaningful time for family and community to celebrate life together and invite the Holy Spirit to bless our children with His presence. Is it an issue of heaven or hell? Do we have to? Of course not; but it is just an example of the life that is found in that rich, ancient root that we have become part of.

Adoption

Instead of the term, "grafted in", which we are somewhat numb to and seems more like a theological term than a practical one, let's think in terms of being adopted. Years ago I took a class on ancient Israel and learned some fascinating things. One of the subjects that I felt was very important for believers in Jesus to understand was adoption. In Roland de Vaux's book, Ancient Israel, Volume 1, he discusses the idea of tribal rites. These rites were kept by many of the ancient desert tribes, including the tribes of Israel. Survival was key because enemies abounded and if your tribe was wiped out, you could be adopted into a larger tribe. To do this you had to renounce the name of your old tribe publicly, and after you did, it was never mentioned again. You then take on the blood and the name of the tribe you are joining, and it is as though your old name and tribe never existed. Their blood is now your blood and family. Their name is now forever yours. Your old identity is remembered no more.

We see an example of this in the person of Caleb. Caleb was from a pagan tribe called the Kenezzites and he was the son of Yephunneth. (Num. 32:12; Joshua 14:6) But he is remembered as from the tribe of Judah. (Num. 13:6; Joshua 15:13) In the book of 1Chron. 2:9, 18, 24, we see Caleb, formerly the son of Yephunneth become the son of Hezron, the son of Peres, the son of Judah. He was adopted into Judah, took the name and the blood and from that point on was only mentioned as from that Israeli tribe. Even Jacob set Joseph's half Egyptian sons, Ephraim and Manassah on his lap… on his loins… symbolizing from that day forward, they would be as though they actually came forth from Jacob's loins… and he blessed them. Wow! Do you see what Romans 8:15 is saying about the "Spirit of adoption" that we can now cry out, "Abba, Father"!

What happens when we receive this spirit and are adopted into the Father's family? We take on the name and the blood! We take on a new identity and a new DNA; as though the old never existed and is never remembered again!!! We are now part of the family of Jesus and **Romans 8: 17** says that we are now *"… joint heirs with Christ…"* Now in that context, let's think about being "grafted in". If a wild, weaker root is grafted into a bigger, stronger one, it now partakes of the life sap, or blood of that new root and takes on the new identity of that tree. We have been adopted into the family of Jesus and His family has characteristics and culture and festivals and traditions and ways of doing life. If we adopt a baby, he or she will not be raised in the ways of their original family but will now take on ours.

Now I have opened a can of worms. You are thinking, "so does that mean we become Jewish"? Yes! No! What kind of answer is that? **Yes**, in the sense that we are born again and adopted into a family that was in existence for 1500 years before Jesus came. **Yes**, our spiritual roots go back to Abraham and our festivals with their rites and ceremonies go back to Moses. **Yes**, the biblical culture and philosophy of tikun olam that the Jews carried and was manifest in Jesus is how we are to live; and **yes**, our Bibles are Jewish with phrases and idioms and cultural references that can only be understood from a Jewish context. **However, I mean no,** if we are talking about the expression of Judaism that has biblical roots and has

I do not believe we have ever seen the expression of what these two streams look like when they are joined together

faithfully carried all the riches of the rites and ceremonies and philosophies of life, but are devoid of the revelation of Jesus as their Messiah. Without Him they are dead and are expressed in the form of rabbinic Judaism that is in as much of an identity crisis as the church is without knowing our Jewish roots. What does it look like then? I don't know because I do not believe we have ever lived in a time before where Jewish people saw that what they carry is about Jesus and the church understands that we are grafted into a Jewish family and culture. I do not believe we have ever seen the expression of what these two streams look like when they are joined together… but I believe we are about ready to.

Ancient Jewish Wedding Ceremony

There are a multitude of meaningful insights that I have gleaned from the Jewish customs and traditions, but as a lover of Jesus, none has impacted me as powerfully as the ancient Jewish wedding ceremony. Once you are familiar with all the different aspects of it, you will see that it is alluded to all through the Old and New Testaments. Being familiar with the ancient wedding customs does more than add richness to our understanding of the family we have been adopted into, it actually opens up and explains the central theme of the Bible and the intense passion of the heart of God for His people. The pattern of the Levitical 23 feasts is in tune with it and references are scattered as clues in almost every (if not every) book of the Bible.

Someone once said to me, "You cannot base your entire theology on one little Jewish custom". I would agree if I could say that I have only found it in one or two scriptures, but I have found it everywhere!! Jesus Himself uses references to wedding customs throughout the gospels and in the book of Revelation. Paul refers to them also in the epistles. So, let's look at the elements to an ancient Jewish wedding and then I will share with you a few personal revelations I had at my son's Jewish wedding 17 years ago. Now put aside your twentieth century western lens of courtship and marriage so you can gain from the ways of the eastern customs and mindset that was prevalent in Jesus' day.

Jewish marriages were usually arranged by the parents of the bride and groom but mainly by the father of the groom. **Jer. 29:6 says, "…take wives for your sons and give your daughters to husbands…"** Once the prospective bride was chosen, the bridegroom to be would go to her parents' home where she lived, taking four important things with him: a skin of wine, a sum of money called a "mohar" or "bride-price", gifts for the bride should she agree, and a marriage contract called a "ketubah". Any young man arriving at a girl's house with these in his possession would be obvious in his intentions.

First the parents of the bride would be summoned and their permission would be sought. If they agreed, the bride was brought out and the hopeful bridegroom would pour a cup of wine known as "the cup of betrothal". If she accepts the proposal, she would say yes by drinking the cup of wine that was set before her. It was at this point that more prominent and wealthy people might include what was known as a "banquet of wine". Guests would be assembled, an elaborate feast would be prepared, and at the head table the bridegroom to be would pour a cup of wine and the proposed bride would be the center of everyone's attention. She would be attired in beautiful clothes to be admired by all and then would dance somewhat playfully, grab the cup as if to drink, then she would put it down again to tease the groom until finally she drank it and everyone cheered.

We see an example of this in the book of Esther, only not in the context of betrothal, but in a gesture by Esther to please and entertain the king in a somewhat alluring way in order to gain his favor. It was probably a banquet of wine that Vashti was invited to by the king to show her off to all his nobles, and her refusal cost her position as queen. There is even a phrase that King Ahasuerus says in *Esther 5:6, "... What is your petition? It shall be granted you. What is your request, up to half the kingdom? It shall be done!"*

It is interesting to note that in the New Testament, after John the Baptist is put in prison by King Herod, that King Herod throws a birthday party for himself. He invited all the dignitaries and nobles and holds a banquet... most likely a banquet of wine. It was in this context that Herodias' daughter seductively danced before the king to gain his favor. She had an evil request to get vengeance against John the Baptist, and her enticing dance pleased the king. Herod says to her, in front of all the esteemed guests, the same thing that King Ahasuerus said to Esther: *"Ask me whatever you want, and I will give it to you...I will give you, up to half my kingdom" (Mark 6:22-23)*. This was not a random saying by King Herod; rather it was a known custom of ancient eastern cultures to hold a banquet of wine to show off the grandeur of your kingdom and the beauty of a bride. I believe these references in scripture are a foreshadowing of a Day when the King of all Kings, Jesus, will return to the earth and hold a banquet to show off the beauty of His bride for all the earth to marvel at. *Song of Songs 2:4 says, "He brought me to the banqueting house, And his banner over me was love."*

Now let's continue with the ancient Jewish wedding customs; I just thought it was important to see that this cup of betrothal was sometimes in the context of a banquet of wine. Either way, once the bride drank this cup, the engagement was official, and the contractual phase of the wedding was initiated. A mohar, or bride price, was paid to the girl's parents and the ketubah, or contract, with the pledge of the groom to care for her was signed. Now they were legally married and would have to go through a divorce to dissolve the marriage. This explains the situation of Joseph and Mary who were legally betrothed when Mary was pregnant with Jesus but the consummation part of the wedding had not yet taken place.

The bridegroom then leaves gifts for the bride as a pledge to return for her in the future. He leaves her so He can go build a bridal chamber on His father's house. It is the place He is preparing to bring her for the second part of the wedding, known as the consummation. When would he be back for her? No one knew but his father. Does this sound familiar? His Father had to inspect the chamber and once it met his specifications, he would release his son to go get his bride. The common saying was, "no man knows the day or hour, only the father". This was the phrase, or idiom, that Jewish people in Jesus' day would understand to be talking about the time when the bridegroom would go to kidnap his bride.

> *no man knows the day or hour, only the father*

Side Note: I cannot resist throwing a little "clue" out here that I will discuss in my teaching on the fall feasts that speak of Jesus' second coming; the phrase, "No man knows the day or hour" is also used in reference to something that takes place during the first fall feast of Yom Teruah!!! It is all so perfect; it will blow your mind! No one could make this stuff up... when you see how all the pieces come together you will feel born again, again!

While the bridegroom was away, the bride spent the time sewing her wedding garments and preparing to be a wife. From the day of her betrothal, she was set apart and was veiled when she went in public. From this day on she was known as, *"...You are not your own. For you were bought at a price." (1Cor. 6:19-20)*. Then, when the groom's father was satisfied that all was in order, usually within a year, the friends of the bridegroom would blow a shofar and proclaim in the streets, "Behold the bridegroom cometh!" And the bridegroom would go forth with a procession to the bride's house, usually at midnight, and "abduct the bride". That is the reason he was called, "the thief in the night" because he came suddenly at an hour unknown to the bride and she had to be watching and living with the expectation that he was coming any minute. Wow! What woman would not love the excitement and intrigue of this romantic custom of her bridegroom coming at an unknown day and hour to snatch her away in the dark and carry her to his bridal chamber! Four men would carry the palanquin or carriage on their shoulders to take the bride back to the groom's house. This was known as the "nissuin", the taking or "catching up" of the bride. Ten virgins carrying tall torches accompanied the bride to the bridal chamber. It was here that the second part of the wedding, called the consummation was performed and it was sealed with another cup of wine appropriately called the cup of consummation. The bride and groom would then enter the bridal chamber or chuppah for seven days to consummate the wedding. The friends of the bridegroom stand at the door and announce their coming out from the chuppah to

she had to be watching and living with the expectation that he was coming any minute.

family and guests that are waiting for the wedding feast to begin!

Jesus the Bridegroom chooses a bride by the will of the Father. **John 15:16 says, "You did not choose Me, but I chose you…"** Following the pattern of an ancient Jewish wedding, Jesus sets up a "banquet of wine" in an upper room the night before He dies. In the context of a traditional Passover meal, He initiates a betrothal ceremony and takes a cup of wine and says, **"…I will not drink of this fruit of the vine from now on until that day when I drink it new with you in My Father's kingdom" (Matt. 26:29).** What day was He alluding to? The day when the second cup of wine is poured, the cup of consummation, that is partaken of in the bridal chuppah! Then in **John 14:1-3**, Jesus says something only a bridegroom would say at his betrothal. He says,

> **"Let not your heart be troubled; you believe in God, believe also in Me. In My Father's house are many mansions; if it were not so, I would have told you. I go to prepare a place for you. And if I go and prepare a place for you, I will come again and receive you to Myself; that where I am, there you may be also".**

Jesus even refers to the tradition that as the Bridegroom, He cannot tell them when He will return to take them to the wedding chuppah because the Father is the One Who decides the right time. He says in **Mark 13:32, "But of that day and hour no one knows, not even the angels in heaven, nor the Son, but only the Father".** Then Jesus tells parables to make sure they understand that although He is going away it is important that they live as a watchful bride; waiting for His return, living set apart for Him, and looking forward to the day when He come again. He tells the story of the ten virgins and we see all the language of a traditional Jewish wedding. The Bridegroom is delayed and then while the

> *although He is going away it is important that they live as a watchful bride*

virgins are waiting, they fall asleep. Then when the shout comes at midnight that the bridegroom is coming, we see that only the ones that had oil (intimacy in their hearts watching and preparing for him to come), could enter the bridal chamber. Again, in Matt.24:42-44 Jesus tells them to stay alert because they will not know what day the Lord is coming. He says to be on the alert because just like a thief in the night (bridegroom that abducts the bride), the Son of Man is coming at an hour when you do not think that He will.

The extravagant bride price that Jesus paid for His bride was His own life. ***1 Peter 1:18-19 says:***

> ***"knowing that you were not redeemed with corruptible things, like silver or gold...but with the precious blood of Christ, as of a lamb without blemish and without spot."***

1 Cor. 7:23 reminds us that we ***"...were bought at a price".*** The gift Jesus left for us was the Holy Spirit in Acts 2, as a guarantee of His return. Now we are to be living for Him, keeping ourselves pure, anticipating His return.

Paul says in *2 Cor. 11:2*,

> *"For I am jealous for you with a godly jealousy. For I have betrothed you to one husband, that I may present you as a chaste virgin to Christ."*

Remember, also, that in John 3:29, John the Baptist, identified himself as the friend of the bridegroom who has the joy of hearing the bridegroom's voice. This is consistent with the traditional job of a friend of the bridegroom who often escorts the groom to the bride's house, then announces with a trumpet blast when the groom is leaving his father's house to go get the bride, and will later announce to the waiting guests that they are coming out of the bridal chamber after the consummation.

There is a good chance that Moses and Elijah appeared with Jesus on the mount of transfiguration as the two friends of the Bridegroom, the two witnesses that are required for a Jewish wedding to be legal. We will see in chapter 6 of this book that Moses was the friend who escorted the bride, Israel, to Mount Sinai to enter into a marriage covenant with the LORD. Likewise, John the Baptist (who had the spirit of Elijah) was the friend who escorted the bride in the New Testament to Jesus. Could it be that these two witnesses were discussing with the Bridegroom the future details of His wedding??? Was it a foreshadowing of the day when Jesus would come out of His wedding chamber with His bride (Joel 2:16), shining like the sun, to be seen by the whole earth?

I am excited to share with you how this verse in Joel relates to one of the fall feasts because it will explain what Jesus meant in Matthew 24:27 that He will come like

71

lightning flashing from the east to the west. Without the understanding of our Hebrew roots, we miss that this is a Jewish idiom that speaks of a festival and also alludes to part of an ancient Jewish wedding!!! Why does Jesus say in Mark 2:19-20 that His disciples do not fast now because their Bridegroom is with them but they will when He is taken away? Because He is about to initiate a betrothal ceremony and then He will go away on a long journey to prepare a place to take them to in the future. While the Bridegroom is away they will fast, yearning and waiting for His return.

Our Son's Wedding

When our son, Ben married Rebekah in 1996, they chose to have a Jewish wedding because of the rich meaning associated with its customs. At the time, I knew nothing about Jewish weddings, and though I am capable of trying to influence our kids with my good ideas, John and I had no part in their decision. Helping Rebekah as she made preparations was where God began to open my eyes to the prophetic picture of the bridal paradigm seen throughout the Bible.

The night before the wedding, the bride and groom go to a mikvah. A mikvah is the Hebrew word for immersion in water, or baptism. Every Jewish community from ancient Israel to today will have one. They are enclosed, private rooms, with steps leading down to a pool of water. The water had to be what was called, "living water", in that it flowed into the pool from an active source of water and also flowed out. The people immerse themselves as a witness watches; a woman is a witness for a woman and a man for a man. There are various reasons for mikvahs in Jewish life and you will notice that in Hebrews 6:2, the writer of Hebrews uses the plural and says, "baptisms". The priests in temple times went in the mikvah to cleanse themselves before their service to the Lord; anyone touching a dead body were washed in the mikvah; women go into the mikvah on the fourteenth day of their menstrual cycle, to wash away the death of an egg that was not fertilized and to be "cleansed" on this day of ovulation where she might conceive new life.

Hundreds of mikvahs were excavated at the Temple Mount in Jerusalem, which explains how the 5,000 that came to the Lord in Acts 2 could all be baptized. The night before a Jewish wedding, the bride and groom both are separately immersed in the mikvah. Before the witness they acknowledge any physical or emotional tie they have ever had to another man or woman before this day. They immerse themselves to cleanse and repent from all ties of their past and are considered "born again", or as newborn babies, on their wedding day. Ben and Rebekah loved the significance of this so they went out to our hot tub separately, with a witness, and were immersed.

Side Note: I cannot resist drawing your attention to something John the Baptist says when he is announcing the coming of Jesus in *John 3:28-29*.

> *"You yourselves bear me witness, that I said, 'I am not the Christ,' but, 'I have been sent before Him.' He who has the bride is the bridegroom; but the friend of the bridegroom, who stands and hears*

him, rejoices greatly because of the bridegroom's voice. Therefore this joy of mine is fulfilled."

In ancient Israel, what we now call a best man at a wedding was called a "shoshbin", or "friend of the bridegroom". He was the one who escorted the bride to the bridegroom and announced his coming. Could it be that as the friend of the Bridegroom, John the Baptist was taking people to a baptism or mikvah of repentance and cleansing before their betrothal? When Moses, as a friend of the Bridegroom, brought the children of Israel to Mt. Sinai for marriage to God, what did he tell them to do? He told them to first cleanse themselves (Ex. 19:10). Was this a mikvah before a wedding? I believe that it was. It is also worth noting that Jewish scholars believe the first shoshbin or friend of the bridegroom was God when He first brought Eve to Adam. It says in **Genesis 2:22** that, **"...He brought her to the man."**

After the mikvah it is traditional for the bride and groom to fast until their wedding the next day. The fast is broken after the ceremony, where before greeting family and guests, the newly married couple are secluded in a room where they eat a small meal and enjoy the first moments alone together. Ben and Rebekah did this as well, and broke their fast with Omi's chicken soup, alone in a secluded room while their guests waited for them to emerge so the party could begin!

The wedding takes place under a "chuppah" or wedding canopy, which represents the groom's household that he is bringing his new bride into. Before the bride is ushered in by her parents, the groom waits under the chuppah for the moment he can extend his hand and bring her into his "household". As she approaches the chuppah, she circles it seven times, cutting off her ties with her parents household, and then takes the grooms hand as he invites her into his. In ancient Israel, the betrothal ceremony was done at the bride's house, and a year later, the consummation ceremony took place at the groom's "house" that he had prepared for her. Today, both ceremonies take place under the chuppah. After the first cup of wine is taken together, the rings are exchanged and the bride's veil remains down. But after the second cup of wine, the veil is removed, the blessings over the couple are pronounced, and they are officially man and wife. After their time of seclusion, the couple joins the celebration.

They are lifted up on chairs, above the others and with dancing and song are paraded around the room for all to see. This is called the "nissuin", the catching up or "catching away" of the bride and groom. They are considered to be a king and queen, crowned on this day and are lifted up; not on earth, not in heaven, but in between heaven and earth where

> *This is called the "nissuin", the catching up (or "catching away") of the bride and groom.*

all eyes can still see them and declare their beauty. With that profound, prophetic picture in mind, consider this verse:

"For the Lord Himself will descend from heaven with a shout, with the voice of an archangel, and with the trumpet of God. And the dead in Christ will rise first. Then we who are alive shall be <u>caught up</u>

together with them in the clouds to meet the Lord in the air. And thus we shall always be with the Lord."

1 Thes. 4:16-17

A Glimpse Into A Future Wedding

The parallels that we can glean from these marriage customs are eye opening to our understanding of what Jesus came to accomplish at His first coming to earth! In fact, the magnitude of the bridal theme that is woven throughout scripture should cause our hearts to leap for joy! Our Greek trained minds that look for systematic theologies and study the Bible as a classroom textbook are at risk of missing the heart language that speaks of divine romance! Bill Johnson, a pastor from Redding, California said, **"One of the greatest tragedies of life is when the Bible is interpreted by those who are not in love"**.

The Bible is the most amazing, epic love story ever written and we are the central focus of God's passionate and jealous love! We have to stay connected to the love story that started in the Garden of Eden in Genesis. Since the day that Satan's deception caused God to lose face-to-face intimacy with the one made in His image… the one created to partner with Him forever… God initiated His plan to send the Redeemer to get back His bride.

He is a Jewish Bridegroom so it was fitting for Him to stay consistent with the traditions of His culture. The disciples were familiar with the love language He was speaking to them and I am sure the impact of His words at that historic Passover meal left them stunned. They were busy jockeying for positions in what they thought was a political takeover, and Jesus was initiating a betrothal ceremony! Sadly, without this Jewish lens to give us understanding, we have reduced this "last supper" to a stiff, often religious ceremony called communion. Not that it isn't important to remember Jesus' death on the cross, but in the context of a betrothal ceremony, there is an added dimension that strengthens our hearts, remembering that "we have been bought with a price" and a bridal chamber awaits us!

They were busy jockeying for positions in what they thought was a political takeover

This is not just a teaching to add to our list of truths to be discussed at our Bible studies. Understanding the festivals, the Sabbath, and the customs and traditions that we have been grafted into gives us understanding of what Jesus is doing right now because they line up with His prophetic timetable and appointment book of what He has already done and what He will do in the future. We know that He has come as suffering servant and paid for His bride. When He said, "It is finished" as He was dying on the cross, He was speaking the words a bridegroom would say to the bride's father after he had paid the full payment of the "mohar" or bride-price.

Right now, at this very minute, Jesus is building a bridal chamber to bring His bride to one day in the future. As He builds, He is praying for us and singing with joyful anticipation for the day called "the gladdening of His heart". It is the day that John got a glimpse of on the Island of Patmos in Revelation 19 and 21. Jesus gave Him a sneak preview of the "apocalypse", meaning "unveiling"... the main attraction at the end of this age... a bride adorned for her Husband, coming out of a marriage chuppah with her king as she is presented together with Him before the gaping mouths of the whole earth!

Understanding from this perspective also lets us know how we are to live while we are waiting… living in community… loving Him together… sharing the things He has spoken to our hearts… rehearsing His appointments with Him so we can remember what He has done for us, and live with anticipation of what He will do in the future. Living as set apart betrothed brides, watching and waiting for the sound of the last trump announcing that the "thief in the night" is on His way to "abduct us" and take us to Himself. Far from dead religion, it is the incentive that sustains our hearts to keep going, keep redeeming, keep loving like He did. The joy that was set before Him so He could endure the cross; the reality of His wedding day … is now the joy set before us!

Another interesting thing to note here is that a high priest was also known as "a thief in the night". Different priests were allotted temple duties and there was one priest designated to stay up all night making sure that the oil lamp, symbolizing the eternal presence of God, did not go out. When the high priest did his rounds, if he caught the priest, who was to be watching, sleeping, he would take his lantern and light the sleeping priest's garments on fire. He would then have to strip off his garments and shamefully run through the streets naked. It is only in this context, that Revelation 3:3-5; 3:18 and Revelation 16:15 makes sense. The two are similar because the point of Jesus making the two references is to say that He is the Bridegroom that will come for His bride at an unexpected hour and He is the High priest that will make sure our light is still burning. In both cases He is urging us to be alert, be ready, and watch for Him to come!

What Advantage Has the Jew

After 2000 years of church history, as Gentile believers we find ourselves asking the logical question: Why were we not aware of or taught our Jewish roots before? When we read scriptures that mention Jewish concepts and Jewish festivals, why did we not ask what seems like the obvious questions. For example, what does Paul mean when he defines Jesus as, "Christ our Passover"? Or why is He "the Lamb of God that takes away the sins of the world"? What is the Feast of Unleavened Bread? What does the term "firstfruits" refer to and what is the Book of Life that is mentioned throughout scripture? All of a sudden, in the first century, we are grafted into a faith that has had momentum for 1500 years and no one is explaining the foundations, defining the terms or asking any questions! The early church was Jewish and they understood the language of their culture that Jesus, Paul and others used.

It is easy to read the New Testament and feel like you must have missed the class or not gotten the handout explaining what all the Jewish terminology and cultural references mean. You find yourself wishing that one of the Gentile believers would have gone up to Peter or Paul and said, *"Look, I have been a pagan my whole life but I fell in love with your Jewish Messiah, Jesus, and decided to follow Him, but I do not have a clue about what you guys believe. You observe festivals that are unknown to me, and use phrases in your teaching like 'living water' and 'last trump', that refer to ceremonies within those feasts that I know nothing about. How can I understand the Bible if I don't know your faith, your culture and your traditions?"* Exactly! We can't.

We know enough to be saved by the blood of Jesus and because of the gift of the Holy Spirit in us we have a teacher that has given us revelation and relationship with Jesus that is glorious, but we have been adopted into a family and culture that is totally foreign to us. I know this personally, because when I married John I became part of a family that was so strange to me and I did not get the rulebook! I had to do things wrong, ask questions, and feel like an outcast for a while, but with time my thinking changed and I began to get it. I think that God, in His supernatural patience, has just been waiting for His Gentile kids to finally humble ourselves and admit that we cannot go any farther in our understanding and revelation without what my husband John, calls "the Sky King decoder ring". There was a T.V. show in the 1950's with a pilot named Sky King and you could only help Sky and his niece Penny solve the mystery if you sent away for your Sky King decoder ring that would let you know the secrets and help you solve the mystery. We need the Sky King decoder ring!

> *We need the Sky King decoder ring!*

We need the Jewish faith and people who carry more than the Old Testament scriptures. "What advantage has the Jew? Much in every way, to them was given…" What were they given? **Numbers 9: 2-3 says,**

> **"Let the children of Israel keep the Passover at its appointed time. On the fourteenth day of this month, at twilight, you shall keep it at its appointed time. According to all its rites and ceremonies you shall keep it."**

They were told to keep the Passover. How? By **"…all the rites and ceremonies…"** They were given to Moses on the mountain who taught the people and they were passed down orally and then recorded in Jewish writings. Where are those found? The language of them is found all through the Bible, but the explanations are not given, they are assumed. An example of this is found in *John 7:37-38*. It says, *"On the last day, that great day of the feast..."* The feast was the Feast of Tabernacles, the last fall feast. In verse 8, Jesus says He is the living water. If you were a Jew in that day, His declaration would not need explanation. They knew that "living water" was associated with a living water ceremony enacted every year during this feast. Also, all the scripture verses in the Old Testament about living water were read for the seven days of the Feast of Tabernacles. Right after this, in John chapter 8, is the story of the woman caught in adultery. The scribes and Pharisees wanted to stone her to death and Jesus bends down and writes in the dust. He says as He is writing, "He who is without sin among you, let him throw a stone at her first"(vs 7). One by one, they walk away. What did Jesus write in the dust? We don't know for sure, but a clue might be in a verse they would have just read that week about living water found in Jeremiah 17:13. It states that if they forsake the fountain of living water, their names shall be written in the dust. Who is the Living Water?

Jesus just announced in *John 7:38* that He was.

> *"Oh LORD, the hope of Israel, All who forsake You shall be ashamed. <u>Those who depart from Me shall be written in the earth,</u> because they have forsaken the LORD, The fountain of living waters."*

81

According to the language of the fall feasts that had just ended, the Jews present with Jesus that day knew the following; on the Feast of Trumpets the greeting is, "May your name be inscribed in the book of life". On Yom Kippur the greeting is, "May your name be sealed for the day or redemption". But when your name is, "written in the dust," you are cursed because your name will be trampled by men's feet and will be blown away by the wind. Jesus was making a profound statement within the context of the fall feasts… and they knew He was speaking to them.

It Is Time For Our Jewish Roots To Be Revealed

The festivals they are commanded to observe are all listed in Leviticus 23 but with very little instructions on how to keep them. I remember early on in my search for Jesus in the festivals, He told me to start observing them but Leviticus 23 was void of details. How do you find out how to do a Passover Seder? Jesus and His disciples did one and they did not need to ask Jesus what to do to prepare for it because they were Jews! They did it according to the rites and order of service passed down through oral teachings and writings from generations before them. And do you know what I discovered? Not only did Jesus fulfill the Word; He also used the customs and language of the festivals, with their traditions and services, to reveal Himself as well!

He also used the customs and language of the festivals, with their traditions and services, to reveal Himself as well!

Remember my encounter when I first saw Him as the afikoman in the Passover Seder? He left clues in all the liturgy of the feasts about Himself and how He was going to come! It is amazing, and without tapping into this rich sap of that ancient Jewish olive tree that Paul says we are grafted into, Romans 11, we will miss so much and will not be able to go on the treasure hunt or find "the Afikoman" hidden throughout the Word. I believe the answer to the question of why we never wondered about the rich olive tree that Paul says we are grafted into is a simple one. It is the same reason why Jewish people have all these amazing scriptures like Isaiah 53 that clearly is about Jesus but they cannot see it! Just like them, we have been supernaturally blinded. We can only "see" at all because He has opened our eyes to see.

He has an appointed time for everything. It is His love story, His screenplay, and He is the writer, producer

> *It is His love story, His screenplay, and He is the writer, producer and director.*

and director. He gets to decide when and how His story unfolds. We are living at a time when He is sharing with His friends this incredible plan of redemption that is found in His festivals; His dramatic rescue mission for all of mankind, the ones He chose to live in an intimate relationship with Him forever. It came first to Abraham's seed but ***Galatians 3 says "...if you are Christ's, then you are Abraham's seed, and heirs according to the promise." (Gal 3:29).*** It has always been in the Father's heart that, through Abraham all the nations of the world would ***"...be blessed." (Gen. 12:2).***

83

The Time of the Promise Draws Near

The book of Exodus tells the story of Jacob's family who came to Egypt as 70 people and became a multitude of millions who became enslaved to Pharaoh for 430 years. It is easy to wonder why it took them 430 years to cry out to God to be released from their bondage, but again, the answer is simple: It was not God's appointed time. *Acts 7:17 says, "But when the time of the promise drew near which God had sworn to Abraham, the people grew and multiplied in Egypt".* Also in God's promise to Abraham in Gen. 15:16 He mentions their time of release will come when the sin of the Amorites is complete. When it was His appointed time for this part of His story to unfold, His people cried out and He came down to deliver them. God's timing is PERFECT.

There is 400 years between Malachi and Matthew. This is known as "the time of silence" because God did not speak through a prophet all those years. It continued from Matthew 1, when Jesus was born, to the time of His ministry at age 30. *Hebrews 1:1-2 says,*

> *"God, who at various times and in various ways spoke in time past to the fathers by the prophets, has in these last days spoken to us by His Son, whom He has appointed heir of all things, through whom also He made the worlds;"*

Silence for 400 years plus 30 years until the beginning of Jesus' ministry is 430 years! It is the exact same time of silence in Exodus. It is so perfect that we cannot take the credit or blame for any of it!

By God's will Joseph was sent into Egypt after being sold into slavery by his jealous brothers. He took on an Egyptian name and dress and was promoted to a position of royalty. When his brothers came to Egypt for provisions during the famine, Joseph was so Egyptian he was unidentifiable to them. But, at the appointed time, he gathered them in a room alone, took off his Egyptian garb and said in Hebrew, *"...I am Joseph your brother, whom you sold into Egypt." (Gen. 45:4)*. Likewise, Jesus, in the third century, took on a gentile form with everything about His Jewish identity removed from Him. God purposely hid Him for 1800 years so all the Gentile nations could come to know Him. But one day soon when He returns to this earth, like Joseph, He will gather His Jewish brothers in Jerusalem, without His Greek identity, and say in Hebrew, *"I am Yeshua, the One Whom you pierced" (Zech. 12:10)*.

Since the rebirth of Israel in 1948 there has been a prophetic shift and the church has had their eyes slowly opened to God's plan and purpose for the land of Israel, for the Jewish people, and a new hunger has emerged to discover our Jewish roots. Did we all of a sudden wake up and have understanding? No! It is getting close to the time God chose for His Jewish brothers to have their eyes open to the revelation that much of what they carry in their Jewish faith is about Jesus, and for the Gentile believers to see that their true identity can only be found in the ancient Jewish root that Paul says we are grafted into.

"For if the firstfruit is holy, the lump is also holy; and if the root is holy, so are the branches. And if some of the branches were broken off, and you, being a wild

olive tree, were grafted in among them,
and with them became a partaker of the
root and fatness of the olive tree, do not
boast against the branches. But if you do
boast, remember that you do not support
the root, but the root supports you."

Rom. 11:16-18

Jew and Gentile Coming Together

When Jewish people have a revelation that Jesus is their Messiah and we have revelation that our identity is found in the Jewish root that supports us, we will express what the Father has always wanted: *"... one new Man..."* Jew and Gentile, *(Eph. 2:15).* We cannot be mad at our church fathers or church leaders for keeping it from us. God has kept it for this time in history to be revealed. He allowed the

> *God has kept it for this time in history to be revealed.*

Jewish people to faithfully carry a treasure box with precious jewels that help us know our Jewish Savior, King, and Bridegroom and gives rich explanation and meaning to our Hebrew Bible. We have been grafted into more than a religion. We are adopted into a Jewish family with a culture and traditions that are rich with meaning and teach us how to live. We are living in a time when Jesus, like Joseph, is removing His Greek exterior and is wanting to reveal to His Jewish and Gentile family, "I am Yeshua."

Once our eyes are opened, we will have eyes to see so many scriptures that we did not understand before because we lacked the Hebraic lens to view them through. There are several idioms and references to Jewish festivals all through the Old and New Testaments that give rich meaning and context to what is being said. Hopefully as you go through these teachings, you will have a foundation on which to go mining for gold on your own. I also hope that you receive the extravagant fortune that faithful Jewish brothers have kept in their "safety deposit box" until this present time when the Father is releasing it to His legitimate, grafted in heirs. Now ask Him for a spirit of revelation and understanding of the true knowledge of Him as you open the box!

"Therefore remember that you, once Gentiles in the flesh—who are called Uncircumcision by what is called the Circumcision made in the flesh by hands—that at that time you were without Christ, being aliens from the commonwealth of Israel and strangers from the covenants of promise, having no hope and without God in the world. But now in Christ Jesus you who once were far off have been brought near by the blood of Christ."

Ephesians 2:11-13

~ Chapter 4 ~

Jesus Keeps His Appointments

"And beginning at Moses and all the Prophets, He expounded to them in all the Scriptures the things concerning Himself."
Luke 24:27

To me, the book of Exodus is a masterpiece and a mystery. Our friend Tim Ruthven, who had a ministry on the importance of a daily quiet-time in the Word, gave me an appreciation for this book as a new believer. As part of Tim's ministry we went through a devotional He wrote called, He Brought Us Out to Bring Us In. Tim taught on the types and shadows found in Exodus, and on the steps God took to deliver His children from Egypt and change their identity. They started as a group of slaves in bondage to Pharaoh (a shadow and type of Satan), in an anti-God culture of Egypt (the world system), were delivered out by the blood of a lamb on their doorposts (Jesus, the Lamb of God), and were taken through the Red Sea (a type of baptism) to be God's holy nation.

Walking with Tim and Jesus through this book the first time gave me an appreciation for the shadows and types that God uses to speak to us all through His Word. Exodus took on an even greater importance to me as we began to take people through the Passover story by celebrating each year in our home. After 38 years of teaching about this festival, I became very familiar with the pattern of deliverance and redemption found in Exodus 12 through 19, and I stayed very focused on the revelation of Jesus that can be experienced for us as believers in these chapters. The perfection of God's word is miraculous as you see how Jesus completely fulfilled the pattern of the spring feasts that are found there; but there is more.

Even after gazing at Exodus and the Leviticus 23 pattern of the festivals for many years, looking for His heart that is found there, I am still gaining new revelations. This past fall I was astounded at what I now see is hidden in the pages of Exodus! I am in absolute awe of what I'm getting a glimpse of that I missed all these years. For a long time I have seen that Moses delivered God's people from bondage, took them through the Red Sea and brought them to a mountain to meet with God in Exodus 19. Now I am seeing that in Exodus 19-40, Moses goes through the pattern of the Leviticus 23 fall feasts as well, leaving clues of the second coming of Jesus!!! Moses walks through the pattern of the feasts, which foreshadows the two comings of the future Messiah, without knowing that God would have him later record them in scripture. After his encounter with God on Mt. Sinai, God would have Moses instruct the people to observe, or "rehearse", them so they would know the time of His visitation. Many scriptures point to Jesus following the pattern of Moses:

"I will raise up for them a Prophet like you from among their brethren, and will put My words in His mouth, and He shall speak to them all that I command Him."

Deut. 18:18

"This is that Moses who said to the children of Israel, 'The Lord your God will raise up for you a Prophet like me from your brethren. Him you shall hear."

Acts 7:37

"And beginning at Moses and all the Prophets, He expounded to them in all the Scriptures the things concerning Himself."

Luke 24:27

The Importance of the Pattern

I have used the term "pattern of the feasts" for many years and I do not want to presume that those who are just beginning to study the biblical festivals know what I am referring to. To me, a pattern is a template you can use to duplicate something. If I see a dress in a magazine that I want to sew, I would go to a fabric store and buy a pattern that is exactly like the one I want. I then would have to follow that pattern precisely to get the desired result. God told Moses to build the tabernacle according to the pattern that He gave to him on Mt. Sinai. He showed Moses the heavenly tabernacle that would one day come to earth. Moses came down from that experience with instructions from God to build a dwelling place for Him that would be a reflection of something glorious that was in heaven. It had colors, dimensions, materials, fragrances and articles to be made and placed within it. This heavenly tabernacle that Moses experienced was very important to God and had a purpose and a function that would be an expression of His heart, and He wanted His people to be part of it.

"And let them make Me a sanctuary, that I may dwell among them. According to all that I show you, that is, the pattern of the tabernacle and the pattern of all its furnishings just so you shall make it."
Ex. 25:8-9

When I refer to the pattern of God's festivals, the same thing is true. The pattern is exact. It has a purpose and function that speaks of *"...things concerning Himself" (Luke 24:27)*. When Moses was on Mt. Sinai, in addition to the pattern of how to build the tabernacle, *Numbers 9:2-3* tells us he was given the pattern of the festivals, made up of rites and ceremonies, which was to be followed as well.

"Let the children of Israel keep the Passover at its appointed time. On the fourteenth day of this month, at twilight, you shall keep it at its appointed time. According to all its rites and ceremonies you shall keep it."

Leviticus 23 lists the feasts, and when they are to be observed throughout the year. The feasts are listed in a particular order, on specific days and months on the Hebrew calendar, because they are the exact blueprints of how the Messiah would come down to earth. He would come in the spring, (the former rain agricultural

> *they are the exact blueprints of how the Messiah would come down to earth*

season in Israel) and walk through the order of the spring feasts like He did at His first coming when He fulfilled His role as suffering Servant. Likewise, He will come the second time in the order of the fall feasts, (the latter rain agricultural season in Israel) and fulfill His role as conquering King. Remember *Hosea 6:3?*

> **"Let us know, Let us pursue the knowledge of the LORD. His going forth is established as the morning; He will come to us like the rain, Like the latter and former rain to the earth."**

Wow! Do you see it? I know I am repeating what I already said in a previous chapter but it took me awhile for the magnitude of this to hit my heart. There is a Hebrew word, "shema" that means "listen or hear so that you can do". One of the central Hebrew prayers recited by Jewish people daily is called the Shema, taken from *Deuteronomy 6:4-9:*

> **"Hear (shema) Israel: The LORD our God, the LORD is one.!" You shall love the LORD your God with all your heart, with all your soul, and with all your strength."**

93

The word means more than just "hear". It is as though God is saying, "STOP!!! Let Me have your undivided attention, because I am about to say something that could mean the difference between life and death!" When Jesus was asked what is the most important commandment, He answered with the Shema and reduced all 613 commandments down to two! He tells them what they were to STOP and pay attention to! He said in *Mark 12:28-30,*

> *"Jesus answered him, "The first of all the commandments is: 'Hear, O Israel, the LORD our God, the LORD is one. And you shall love the LORD your God with all your heart, with all your soul, with all your mind, and with all your strength.' This is the first commandment. And the second, like it, is this: 'You shall love your neighbor as yourself.'"*

Side Note: After typing this verse, the Holy Spirit drew my attention to the words, "you shall". All of a sudden I saw it, not so much as a command, but a prophecy from the Lord. He is speaking to His people proclaiming what will surely come to pass one day. He is saying to them, "One day, I am going to come with a mighty move of My Spirit and take the dullness from your hearts to see Who I fully am. When that day comes, you shall love Me!!!

What I am feeling as I am about to talk about the pattern that Moses walked the children of Israel through in Exodus 12 to 19 is this: Shema! Listen! STOP!!! Pay attention!!! The reality of this pattern is absolutely pivotal in

94

understanding the whole Bible!!! Ask for a spirit of revelation to see how miraculous these events are in Exodus and how astounding it is that God set His plan of redemption in motion that began in Exodus and is finished in Revelation when a perfect bride comes down adorned for her husband. It is huge! It is impossible for me to give you every detail because the subject on the pattern of redemption is a book in itself! I am just trying to give you a glimpse; the very beginning of some insight into the glory of this pattern that He is revealing so you can begin looking at it for yourself. If I do not communicate it so that it makes sense, spend time with it until the Holy Spirit reveals to you the enormity of its importance.

From the time that Adam and Eve sinned against God and were expelled from the Garden of Eden, God has had a focused vision of redemption. He set forth a plan to get back His intimate partner and to restore fallen earth and bring vindication against Satan who stole it all from Him. He addressed Satan in Genesis 3:15, warning him that there would be One coming to bruise his head. This "One" that He was referring to was the future Messiah we now know is Jesus. The plan went into action and will keep moving on schedule until that day in the age to come when the earth will once more be perfect. Satan and evil will be removed, and Jesus, with His Bride, will present this gift of a restored earth to the Father. With the earth holy once more, like it was in the Garden of Eden before the fall, His throne can once more come down. There is no power on earth or in Hell that can stop it. God, of course, could have accomplished it by Himself, but He chose to have human partners in His mandate of redemption. Rabbi Irving

Greenberg, in his book, The Jewish Way, affirms that from a Jewish viewpoint, this is true. He says,

> **"The Jewish religion if founded on the divine assurance and human belief that the world will be perfected... but the final, ideal state will not be bestowed upon humans by some miraculous divine fiat. According to classic Judaism, God alone is the divine ground of life but God has chosen a partner in the perfection process. The ultimate goal will be achieved through human participation." (p. 18,19)**

We learned in chapter two of this book that this assignment given to the Jewish people by God is called, "tikun olam", "repairing the world". God chose one man, Abraham, who was His faithful friend and told him that through his heir would come great multitudes.

> *"And the LORD said, "Shall I hide from Abraham what I am doing, since Abraham shall surely become a great and mighty nation, and all the nations of the earth shall be blessed in him?"*
> *Gen. 18:18*

God also told Abraham that the children of Israel would be in bondage for 400 years.

> *"Then He said to Abram, 'Know certainly that your descendants will be strangers in a land that is not theirs, and will serve*

them, and they will afflict them four hundred years. And also the nation whom they serve I will judge; afterward they shall come out with great possessions."'

Gen. 15:13-14

We now find ourselves in the book of Exodus and some of the things that the LORD spoke to Abraham are being fulfilled. They have become a great multitude and they have been in bondage in a foreign land for over 400 years. It is time. What was it time for? It was time for the fulfillment of God's words to Abraham that had been moving forward since they were put in motion in Genesis 3. God was giving Abraham a sense of destiny for the promised seed that would come forth from his union with Sarah. His heirs would be in bondage to a great nation, but their deliverance would become a pattern of a future messianic redemption that would one day include deliverance and salvation for the whole world! The steps that God had Moses lead the children of Israel through; to

It is the plan of redemption that is the New Testament gospel!

save them from slavery, deliver them from bondage, redeem them through the water that brought judgment to their enemies and then take them to a mountain for marriage, is not just a good Bible story. It is the plan of redemption that is the New Testament gospel! That is what I am going to show you by the end of this chapter.

Remember, there are steps the children of Israel walked through in Exodus 12-19. When they were on the journey from Egypt to Mt. Sinai they had no idea that they were actually walking out the Leviticus 23 feasts that would soon be given to Moses when he met with God on that

97

mountain. They walked out the pattern and Moses recorded in writing the feasts of the LORD that corresponded to the four steps of redemption that they had just unknowingly walked through! They rehearsed each one of these festivals for the next 1500 years so they would be so familiar with them that when their Messiah came to fulfill them as suffering servant and conquering King, they would not miss His visitation to earth. God kept saying over and over, "Remember, I am the God of Abraham, Isaac and Jacob Who brought you out of Egypt with a mighty outstretched hand." They rehearsed (and still do) their deliverance by the blood of a lamb and redemption through the water. They re-enacted their identity change from slaves to sons to priests to brides, every year, every spring, for 1500 years. Still, most of

> *from slaves to sons to priests to brides, every year, every spring, for 1500 years*

them missed the time of His first coming when He became the Passover lamb at Passover, was buried on the Feast of Unleavened Bread, was raised from the grave on the First Fruits of the Barley Harvest, and poured out His Spirit at the Feast of Weeks, ("Shavuot" in Hebrew, "Pentecost" in Greek).

Jesus perfectly kept His spring appointments; but the love story does not stop at the first coming of Jesus. He has three more appointments to keep on His appointment book. They are the fall feasts that are the pattern of His second coming to earth as conquering King. If you read the progression in Leviticus 23, they are listed as, Feast of Trumpets, Day of Atonement and the Feast of Tabernacles. Remember the mandate given to the Jews on Mount Sinai was to be a light to the nations to fulfill God's promise to Abraham: ***"Through you, all the nations of***

See the earth will be blessed"

the earth will be blessed"(Gen. 22:18). Their assignment was to be co-redeemers bringing "tikun olam", healing to the world, with God as His covenant partner, until one day the conquering King Messiah would come and rid the earth of evil so God's throne could come down. That is why Jewish people do not talk about heaven. They are walking on a pattern of redemption with God, which is found in the biblical feasts, and their eternal future is ruling and reigning with Him on a redeemed earth that becomes Paradise once more. Contrary to this, Christianity often sees the first coming of Jesus as a means to live eternity in heaven. Rabbi Greenberg, in His book, <u>The Jewish Way</u> made an interesting observation about this. He said,

> **"They (Christians) translated the concept of messianic redemption into a state of personal salvation, thus removing it from the realm of history...the true messiah was not in the external physical world, but in the internal spiritual world. In coming up with this solution, they were acting on the Jewish Exodus model but resolving its tensions in a manner that eventually turned them away from Judaism." (p.37)**

In other words, we have not been connected to the Hebrew calendar where His appointments are found. We have lost the blueprint of His plan of redemption. Jesus came the first time to redeem a bride and get her ready for His return. He is coming to earth the second time to return for His bride, clean up the planet and establish His Kingdom on

> *We have lost the blueprint of His plan of redemption*

earth where He will rule with His people forever. We are part of this whole gospel... this epic screenplay... played out in real time in history... walking connected with Jew and Gentile in community together with Him until that final redemption comes. We have to get back on the conveyor belt, on His biblical calendar with Him and the Jewish people, rehearsing His "moedim", appointments, until He returns.

I know I am repeating myself again and again but I feel the Lord wants me to say it repeatedly. The steps that

FIRST
MOSES...
THEN
JESUS

Moses walked through as he led the children of Israel out of bondage, out of Egypt, through the Red Sea and then to a mountain, was THE EXACT SAME PATTERN THAT THE MESSIAH WOULD ONE DAY WALK OUT IN REAL TIME ON THIS EARTH! FIRST MOSES... THEN JESUS, a Prophet like Moses (Deut. 18:18), would walk out the exact same steps to get a bride., I feel to repeat that again. THE PURPOSE OF HIS PLAN HAS ONE GOAL: TO GET A BRIDE. Once you see that, the whole Bible, as well as our whole purpose as believers in Jesus, comes into focus. God did not want His people saved and delivered out of Egypt for the sake of freedom alone. He led a people out to take them to a mountain to enter into a marriage covenant. When we marry, we become one with that person and our callings and life goals merge together and become one. Once in covenant with God in Exodus 19, the children of Israel are given one assignment as partners with Him. Their new mandate is to now do what He does. What does God do? He intercedes, He redeems, He repairs, and He restores all that has been defiled by the enemy, and He will continue to do that until all people,

100

places and things are made new. The Sermon on the Mount that Jesus gave in the New Testament was a reminder to Jews of that mandate. This is the mandate that Romans 11 says that we have been grafted into. I know I am repeating what I already told you in chapter two but this pattern of redemption is so vital to understand.

Moses wrote down the Leviticus 23 Feasts of the LORD according to this pattern He had walked them through. How ironic, that God made this seemingly dull, twenty-third chapter in a book of the Bible that seems burdened with law and boring ritual and made it the key chapter in the whole of scriptures! I believe He had it hidden here to keep it safe for 2,000 years of church history, knowing that as Gentiles, we would

> *I believe He had it hidden here to keep it safe for 2,000 years of church history*

skim through it (if we read it at all), and see absolutely nothing that could possibly be relevant for the church today! Who knew that Leviticus 23 would be the chapter that contained a plan of how the Messiah was coming to earth that has been hidden from Jews and Christians alike but now is being revealed to those who love Him!

Before we get into my explanation of how Jesus fulfilled the Exodus 12-19 events that became the Leviticus 23 feasts, I need to leave you with another very important thought. It is another tidbit that you must understand. The first coming of Jesus was glorious beyond words. His death on the cross overwhelms me to think about and is beyond comprehension. However, the gospel does not end with His death and resurrection. As the church, we have made what He accomplished at His first coming to earth the beginning and end of salvation and redemption. It is not the end and our only job as believers is not to get as many people to heaven as we can in our lifetime. That is a part of our assignment but it is bigger than that. We have been grafted into the same mandate that the Jewish Bride received on Mt. Sinai. As His betrothed Bride we are now co-redeemers with Him. We are to live being light and salt, loving God and loving others and bringing life and healing and salvation to all who need it. Jews focus on restoring this fallen world because that is their God-given assignment that has now become ours. We cannot accomplish it as solo believers. This walk with the Lord was only meant for community and families. *Exodus 19:2 says, "Israel camped before the mountain."* The word "camped" in this verse is a singular verb. They were as one man coming before God on that mountain.

One time during worship years ago, we were singing a song from Romans about running the race, keeping your eye on the prize and I pictured this lonely marathon runner by himself giving it his all to make it to the finish line. I felt the Holy Spirit whisper to me, "It is a relay race, not a marathon, and everyone participates together." Then I saw it. We all get a turn to "carry the baton" in our lifetime and then we get the privilege of passing it on to the next person, or the next generation, in line. The people that went before us are on the sidelines cheering us on to keep going hard, keep going towards the prize that, in the end, we all receive together. God gave me a scripture that has become my prayer concerning my "baton" or message that I am carrying. *Psalm 71:17,18* says,

"Oh God, You have taught me from my youth; and to this day I declare Your wondrous works. Now also when I am old and grayheaded, O God, do not forsake

me, until I declare Your strength to this generation, Your power to everyone who is to come."

We are co-redeemers, redeeming as many as we can, bringing as much light as we can wherever we go. We are contributors in our generation; in our workplaces, in our homes, in our families, in our communities… in life, where God partners with us and in us. We are part of a much bigger story than ourselves but our part, however big or small it may seem, is vital. We have injuries and setbacks and enemies that try to trip us up and urge us to quit but we have to keep listening to the multitudes that went before us who are on the sidelines saying, "Keep going! You can do it! Don't quit now! You are almost to the finish line!" The reality is that there are more for us than against us…hosts of angels and "a great cloud of witnesses" who had the outrageous courage when it was their turn to run the race, to keep following Jesus… to believe and to pass the testimony of their faith… their baton, on to us.

The entire gospel from beginning to end can be found in Exodus 12 through 40 and in Leviticus 23! We will only go through spring feasts in this book. We will look at the fall feast pattern in my second book where I can only speculate and wonder since those feasts are prophetic and yet to come. By the time we are finished, I hope you are as stunned at the perfection of this plan and vision as I have been all these years. I will begin by laying a brief foundation

> *The entire gospel from beginning to end can be found in Exodus 12 through 40 and in Leviticus 23!*

of a Hebrew day and how and why God changed the Hebrew calendar in Exodus 12 so we can follow along with the Israelites journey out of Egypt.

The Mystery of the Sun and the Moon

Genesis 1:1 begins with, ***"In the beginning God created the heaven and the earth."*** Then the chapter unfolds the order of His creation. There are two key things to not only understanding the pattern of the festivals, but in understanding biblical, Hebrew concepts. The first thing we have to see is that a biblical day begins at sundown and goes to sundown the following day. We see this all through chapter one.

> ***"God called the light Day, and the darkness He called Night. So the evening and the morning were the first day."***
> ***Gen. 1:5***

This is so consistent with the theme of redemption that runs through all of Hebrew thinking. Light always triumphs over darkness.

> ***"In Him was life, and the life was the light of men. And the light shines in the darkness, and the darkness did not comprehend (or overpower) it."***
> ***John 1:4-5, parenthesis added***

So a Hebrew day begins with light as the sun goes down and ends in light as the sun goes down the following day. In contrast, our day on the Gregorian calendar (the most widely used civil calendar) begins at the darkest hour; midnight, and ends the following day at the same dark hour yet again, when there is the least amount of light.

The second thing I want to point out is the biblical importance of the sun and the moon and their purpose. As I mentioned in chapter 2, the Hebrew word for festivals in Leviticus 23:2 is "moedim", meaning "appointments". **Genesis 1:14** says,

> ***"Then God said, "Let there be lights in the firmament of the heavens to divide the day from the night; and let them be for signs and seasons, and for days and years;"***

The Hebrew word for signs in this verse is "owth", and means a signal; like Morse code sending a signal or warning. The Hebrew word for seasons is also "moedim", the same word for feasts or appointments! So God is saying that He put the sun and the moon in the sky to signal to earth concerning His coming! The Hebrew calendar that God's appointments are on is lunar, (and solar, but you will have to study that on your own) and is set according to the new moon of the Hebrew month Tishri. This will be especially important when we look at the fall festivals but for now, I just want you to have a basic understanding of God's calendar for the sake of showing you how Jesus perfectly walked out the pattern of the Leviticus 23 spring feasts.

The Hebrew Calendar: Two First Months

Look on the chart in **Appendix E** and you will see the biblical calendar. You will see the 12 Hebrew months paralleled with our Gregorian calendar. I would encourage you to do a more in-depth study on your own. It is not that understanding the Hebrew calendar is so hard, it is just that it is foreign to us if we have lived our whole lives on our familiar, Gregorian calendar. I have to inject a personal story about the calendar that might encourage you.

Eight years ago I was teaching some good friends of ours, Jess and Alice, about the festivals. We came to this part I am sharing with you now about the Hebrew calendar and Jess was confused. I tried to explain it to him with charts and long explanations, but he could not get breakthrough. A few months went by and one day I ran into Jess and he came up to me with tears streaming down his face and said, "I get it." I said, "You get what?" He said, "The calendar. It just came to me by revelation from the Lord." Much of what I am sharing concerning our Hebrew roots is unfamiliar. Do what I did. Do what Jess did. Ask for revelation from the Holy Spirit. He is a really good teacher.

Jewish people believe the world was created on Tishri 1. If you look at the calendar in **Appendix E**, you will see that it begins during our month of September/October. It is considered the first day of the Jewish New Year. This is the day Jews believe God spoke the world into existence and it is called Rosh Hashanah, meaning "head of the year". The new moon of Tishri 1 sets the civil/secular calendar for the rest of the lunar cycle of months. But if you read in Ex.12:1, God gives His people a new first month creating a religious/sacred order to the existing calendar. This new first month, known as Nissan or Aviv, marks the beginning of their dramatic deliverance out of Egypt. Imagine this; after approximately 2500 years of human history, it's as if God comes down, sets His affections on a people and says,

> It's time to walk in step with the rhythms of heaven

> *"Come up higher... I want you with Me where I am. It's time to walk in step with the rhythms of heaven. It's time for my Lev. 23 pattern of appointed times to be revealed."*

On this holy calendar the month of Tishri now becomes the 7th month instead of the first month. As a result, His people now have one calendar and two first months. Now let's read the verse:

> **"Now the LORD spoke to Moses and Aaron in the land of Egypt, saying, "This month (Aviv, known as Nissan after the Babylonian captivity) shall be your beginning of months; it shall be the first month of the year to you.""**
> **Ex. 12:1-2, parenthesis added**

So, what God is saying to the children of Israel is, "From now on Tishri will still be the first month on your civil calendar, but now I am beginning a new first month for My sacred calendar, to set apart the secular from the sacred and mark the day I began to woo you and begin My courtship with you so I could take you as My covenant partner." In other words, just like there is a day that we are born into this world that we celebrate; there is also a date when we were born again. The children of Israel from Exodus 12:1 now had a religious first month and God's appointments were aligned to this. Tishri remained the first month on the secular calendar to commemorate the birthday of the world, but it became the seventh month on the religious calendar, and the date of the first fall feast of Yom Teruah (Feast of Trumpets). I want to introduce to you the idea of two theaters. Instead of seeing a flat one dimensional calendar, think two dimensions, heaven and earth, going on simultaneously. **(See Appendix D)** I don't expect you to fully understand this right now but I promise that if you ask for a spirit of revelation, you will see the magnitude of the tender gesture that came from God's heart to mark the season of His betrothal.

God's Courtship to Israel Begins

We find in the book of Exodus God's plan to deliver His chosen bride from her captivity as He releases the time for their divine romance to begin. In case you think I am romanticizing a portion of scripture, to prove my point of view let me remind you of God's perspective of what was taking place in His heart when He brought them out of Egypt. He says in *Jeremiah 2:2*, when He is lamenting over an unfaithful bride:

> *"Moreover the word of the LORD came to me, saying, "Go and cry in the hearing of Jerusalem, saying, 'Thus says the LORD: "I remember you, The kindness of your*

youth, The love of your betrothal, When you went after Me in the wilderness, In a land not sown."

Exodus 12 is remembered by God and the Jewish people as the time that His courtship with them began. I want to share a quote from a Jewish website that speaks of this reality:

"**During the Shabbat of Passover week it is customary to read the ancient "love song" of King Solomon called Shir Ha-Shirim (שִׁיר הַשִּׁירִים), or the "Song of Songs." In Jewish tradition, since Passover marks the time when our "romance" with God officially began, the sages chose this song to celebrate God's love for His people…" The Song is usually interpreted as an allegory of the love affair between God and His people. The Beloved (representing God) therefore says, "As a lily among the thorns, so is my love for you among the daughters;" and the maiden (representing God's people) replies, "Like an apple tree among the trees of the forest, so is my beloved among the young men. I delight to sit in his shade, and his fruit is sweet to my taste" (Song 2:2-3). The Jewish scholar Maimonides argued that the song was intended to teach about ahavat HaShem (אַהֲבַת יהוה), The whole world attained its supreme value only on the day** when the Song of Songs was given to Israel" (Mishnah Yadayim 3:5). Rashi agrees and therefore states that all the references to King Solomon (שְׁלֹמֹה) in the song refer to the LORD, the King of the Universe who creates peace (שָׁלוֹם) in His high places. Soren Kierkegaard likens the Song to a parable about the disguise of love, the tender passion that is hidden so as to elevate the identity of the beloved. Rashi interpreted the song as an allegory of a young and beautiful woman (the "Shulamite") who becomes engaged to and then marries a king. However, some time later, the woman became unfaithful to him, and the king then sent her into exile to live "as a widow." Despite his heartache, the king's love for her remained constant, and he secretly watched over her and protected her from "behind the shutters." When she finally resolved to return and to be faithful to him alone, the king took her back, with a love that was fully restored. For Rashi, the Jewish people were "engaged" to God when He took them out of Egypt. At that time, Israel pledged love and loyalty to God alone at Sinai (a type of "chuppah" or marriage canopy), but later proved to be unfaithful, first with the sin of the Golden Calf, and then through subsequent acts of infidelity. Indeed, her infidelity proved to be so great that God reluctantly sent her into exile. **According to Rashi, the opening verse, "Let him kiss me with the kisses of his mouth, for your love is better than wine" (Song 1:2), is allegorically spoken by Israel in her exile, as she pines away for the former intimacy she once enjoyed with God."**

"I am my beloved's and my beloved is mine; he grazes among the lilies." (Song 6:3)

(Hebrew4Christians, Shir Ha Shirim)

How Jesus Fulfilled the Spring Feasts

Follow along with me now beginning in Exodus 12:1 and we will trace the pattern of the feasts that Moses walked the children of Israel through when they were delivered from Egypt. I have also added an additional timeline in **Appendix F** for you to reference. Keep in mind they did not know they were establishing a pattern for the set feasts that their ancestors would be following for millenniums to come. They were just doing life and were experiencing the unfolding drama of their journey from slavery to freedom.

They had heard about God in stories from their fathers, but now God was showing them He was real and He came down in His great power manifesting supernatural signs and wonders. The nation where they had lived as slaves for 430 years was being destroyed all around them. I doubt if they understood the magnitude of the prophetic moment they were in the midst of, and certainly could not have known the precedent that God was establishing in the timing of these events for their future. I do not believe Moses understood either. When he met with God on top of Mt. Sinai, he was given the pattern of the feasts later written down in Leviticus 23, and was taught how to observe them. Then, astonishingly, 1500 years later, Jesus came, walked out the same pattern found in Exodus 12-19 and kept the feasts according to the rites and ceremonies given to Moses. Keep in mind that these ceremonies were handed down through the generations and kept alive until the time of Jesus and much of their liturgy is still observed today. Now let's walk through the first Passover, Feast of Unleavened Bread, Firstfruits and the Feast of Weeks with Moses and the children of Israel and then see how Jesus fulfilled them 1500 years later.

The first command given to Moses is found in **_Exodus 12:3_**.

10th of Aviv: 1500 BC

"Speak to all the congregation of Israel, saying: 'On the tenth of this month every man shall take for himself a lamb, according to the house of his father, a lamb for a household".

Every household had to select a lamb, and tie it outside their dwelling. They would keep it there to examine it and to make sure it had no imperfections. It would be tied outside their doorways for four days, and the children would probably get attached to it.

10ᵗʰ of Aviv: 1500 years later

Here we are 1500 years later ready to follow Jesus through the same Passover season that we just saw Moses and the children of Israel experience. In the same way that the Passover lamb was taken on the 10ᵗʰ of Aviv and tied outside their houses to be examined for 4 days in the book of Exodus, so too, in Jesus' day the public Passover lamb was taken into Jerusalem to the temple court to be examined for 4 days. Why is it so important to see that Jesus came into Jerusalem on the 10th? Because it was on this day that the temple priests, accompanied by singers and musicians, would bring in the public Passover lamb into Jerusalem from the fields of Bethlehem.

Side Note: From my understanding of historical books and Jewish commentaries, the priests would bring in a Passover lamb for Israel as a nation. This lamb was carried into Jerusalem by a priest and could be viewed publicly in the temple court where it was tethered and examined for four days. In addition, each family would take a lamb for their household (at least 10 people to a lamb, so it sometimes would include guests to make ten or more). These lambs would be slaughtered on Aviv 14 as well and then roasted and eaten in their households.

As the priest and his procession walked down the hill into Jerusalem, the people would gather in great crowds and, lay palm branches on the road as they walked by. The musicians and singers would be singing the Hallel (praise) from Psalm 118:

"Save now, I pray, O LORD; O LORD, I pray, send now prosperity. Blessed is he who comes in the name of the LORD! We have blessed you from the house of the LORD. God is the LORD, And He has given us light; Bind the sacrifice with cords to the horns of the altar. You are my God, and I will praise You; You are my God, I will exalt You. Oh, give thanks to the LORD, for He is good! For His mercy endures forever."

Ps. 118:25-29

In the midst of this yearly celebration of bringing in the Passover lambs to Jerusalem on the 10th of Aviv, THE Passover Lamb, Jesus, was descending in their midst. Those who knew He was the Messiah laid palm branches before Him as He rode on the donkey into Jerusalem to become the suffering Servant that would take away the sins of the world. Kings of Israel rode into Jerusalem on a donkey when they were announcing peace. They rode in on a white horse when they were announcing war. It was not yet time for Jesus to come on a white horse as conquering King, but one day in the future, this Day will also come.

As the Passover lamb was tied to a post in the temple court to be examined for blemishes for four days, so too Jesus was examined by the Sadducees and Pharisees during these four days before His death and was asked His hardest questions. (Luke 20: 1-47; Matt. 22:15-46; Mark 12: 13-34)

Since we know the Passover lambs are killed on the 14th, we can count back on the calendar below six days from the 14th and see that Jesus was having dinner at

Lazarus' house Saturday the 9th of Aviv. We can infer this from *John 12:1-2* where it says,

> *"Then six days before the Passover Jesus came to Bethany, where Lazarus was who had been dead, whom He had raised from the dead. There they made Him a supper; and Martha served, but Lazarus was one of those who sat at the table with Him."*

Keep in mind that a Hebrew day goes from sundown to sundown. Now look at my chart below;

AVIV

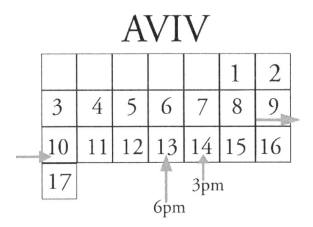

					1	2
3	4	5	6	7	8	9
10	11	12	13	14	15	16
17						

6pm   3pm

There is a weekly ceremony at the conclusion of the Sabbath on Saturday at sundown called Havdalah. So, I believe Jesus was at Mary, Martha and Lazurus' house Saturday night having a meal and celebrating this Havdalah ceremony. In this ceremony a cup of wine symbolizing the joy of the Lord is poured in the cup until its overflowing. A candle with four wicks is lit and extinguished in the cup of wine. Then, a spice box with fragrant oils and spices mixed together is passed around for everyone to smell so they will remember the delight of the Sabbath. I don't think it's a coincidence that this evening when Jesus was with them that Mary took a pound of costly oil and anointed Jesus's feet causing the room to be filled with its fragrance. I believe this fragrance lingered on His garments and body as He hung on the cross reminding Him of Mary's extravagant love for Him helping Him focus on, *"...the joy set before Him so He could endure the cross" (Heb 12:2).*

The 10th of Aviv began at sundown on the 9th. Jesus probably spent the night and we see from the scripture below He went to Jerusalem, still the 10th of Aviv.

> *"The next day a great multitude that had come to the feast, when they heard that Jesus was coming to Jerusalem, took branches of palm trees and went out to meet Him, and cried out: "Hosanna! 'Blessed is He who comes in the name of the LORD!' The King of Israel!"*
>
> *John 12:12-13*

So from this we conclude that Jesus was at Lazarus's house on the 9th and 6 days later on the 14th He died on the cross at 3 pm.

14ᵗʰ of Aviv: 1500 BC

Passover

> *"Your lamb shall be without blemish, a male of the first year. You may take it from the sheep or from the goats. Now*

you shall keep it until the fourteenth day of the same month. Then the whole assembly of the congregation of Israel shall kill it at twilight."

Ex. 12:6

After examining it for four days they were to kill the little lamb at twilight. The Hebrew word for twilight is "bain arbayim", which means "between the evenings". To explain further a Jewish day is divided up into four, three-hour prayer times:

- 6 a.m. until 9 a.m. --------------minor morning oblation

- 9 a.m. until 12 noon -----------major morning oblation

- 12 noon until 3 p.m. -----------minor evening oblation

- 3 p.m. until 6 p.m. -------------major evening oblation

So, 3 p.m. was known as "between the evenings", or twilight.

In Exodus 12:8-9, we are told the lamb was to be roasted before sundown. According to the tractate Pesahim in the Mishnah (a Jewish book that is the oral interpretation of the law), the lamb was roasted on an upright pomegranate stick. This pomegranate stick is representative of the tree upon which Jesus died. The lamb was to be gutted, and its intestines were to be removed and put over its head. Thus, the lamb is referred to as the "crowned sacrifice."

14ᵗʰ of Aviv: 1500 years later

9 a.m. = 3ʳᵈ hour

According to the custom of ancient Israel that followed the pattern of Exodus 12, after four days of examination in the Temple court the Passover lamb was killed. On Aviv 14, the Passover lamb for the nation was moved from the temple court and taken to the altar of sacrifice in the Temple at the 3ʳᵈ hour. We saw from the prayer times listed above, the 3ʳᵈ hour = 9 a.m. The lamb would be tied here awaiting execution until the 9ᵗʰ hour, which is 3 p.m. This corresponds to the scripture that says Jesus was nailed to the cross at the 3ʳᵈ hour, or 9 a.m.

Mark 15:25: "Now it was the third hour, and they crucified Him."

3 hours of darkness

Matt. 27:45: "Now from the sixth hour until the ninth hour there was darkness over all the land."

3 p.m. = 9ᵗʰ hour

The priest kills the Passover lamb in the Temple according to Exodus 12:6 at the 9ᵗʰ hour "between the evenings", or 3 p.m. and the High priest proclaims, "It is finished". This term would be said by the priest in the Temple at the conclusion of the daily peace offering as well as the various special festival offerings.

Jesus breathes His last and cries: "It is finished".

> *"So when Jesus had received the sour wine, He said, "It is finished!" And bowing His head, He gave up His spirit."*
> *John 19:30*

As The Passover Lamb, Jesus perfectly fulfilled the Exodus 12:6 pattern of redemption. In addition, He became all the offerings mentioned in Leviticus 1-7, doing away with them forever. *Hebrews 10:11-14* says:

> *"And every priest stands ministering daily and offering repeatedly the same sacrifices, which can never take away sins. But this Man, after He had offered <u>one sacrifice</u> for sins forever, sat down at the right hand of God, from that time waiting till His enemies are made His footstool. For by <u>one offering</u> He has perfected forever those who are being sanctified."*

It is also worth noting here that after a Jewish bridegroom had paid the bride price or mohar to the girl's father. A parchment would be stamped with the words: "Paid in full." In light of these things, Jesus' proclamation, "It is finished" is packed with meaning.

Now it is important to see the scriptures proving that Jesus died at the 9th hour to perfectly fulfill Exodus 12:6.

"And about the ninth hour Jesus cried out with a loud voice, saying, "Eli, Eli, lama sabachthani?" that is, "My God, My God, why have You forsaken Me?"

Matt. 27:46

"Now when the sixth hour had come, there was darkness over the whole land until the ninth hour. And at the ninth hour Jesus cried out with a loud voice, saying, "Eloi, Eloi, lama sabachthani?" which is translated, "My God, My God, why have You forsaken Me?" Some of those who stood by, when they heard that, said, "Look, He is calling for Elijah!" Then someone ran and filled a sponge full of sour wine, put it on a reed, and offered it to Him to drink, saying, "Let Him alone; let us see if Elijah will come to take Him down." And Jesus cried out with a loud voice, and breathed His last."

Mark 15:33-37

We conclude therefore, that Jesus perfectly fulfilled Leviticus 23:5 and became the Passover lamb according to the instructions given in Exodus 12.

15ᵗʰ of Aviv: 1500 BC

Feast of Unleavened Bread

"On the fourteenth day of the first month at twilight is the LORD's Passover. And on the fifteenth day of the same month is the Feast of Unleavened Bread to the LORD; seven days you must eat unleavened bread. On the first day you shall have a holy convocation; you shall do no customary work on it. But you shall offer an offering made by fire to the LORD for seven days. The seventh day shall be a holy convocation; you shall do no customary work on it.' "

Lev. 23:5-8

After killing the Passover lamb at twilight on the 14th, they were to put the blood on the doorposts (Ex 12:7). Then they were to roast the lamb, eat it with unleavened bread and bitter herbs (Ex 12:8), and at sundown, it turned to the 15th.

"In one house it shall be eaten; you shall not carry any of the flesh outside the house, nor shall you break one of its bones."

Ex. 12:4

"And it came to pass, on that very same day, that the Lord brought the children of Israel out of the land of Egypt according to their armies."

Ex. 12:51

"And Moses took the bones of Joseph with him, for he had placed the children of Israel under solemn oath, saying, "God will surely visit you, and you shall carry up my bones from here with you."

Ex. 13:19

15ᵗʰ of Aviv: 1500 years later

Jesus died at 3 pm on the 14th of Aviv and it was preparation day for the Passover. At sundown (around 6p.m.) it would become the 15ᵗʰ, the Feast of Unleavened Bread. Since this feast was known as a "high Sabbath", or "Shabbaton", different than the weekly Sabbath, they had to hurry and get His body down.

Side Note: By the first century the term "Passover" implied the day of the 14ᵗʰ when the lamb was killed as well as the seven days of unleavened bread. Sometimes these eight days were called "Unleavened Bread" and include the day of Passover. It is the same today. When Jewish people say Passover is coming, they mean the whole eight days of both festivals. When you see the term "preparation day" it can be referring to the day before Passover which would be the 13ᵗʰ of Aviv or the day before the Feast of Unleavened Bread which would be the 14ᵗʰ. Jesus would have eaten a Passover meal on the evening when the 13ᵗʰ, (our

Wednesday) turned to the 14th. The next morning, still the 14th until sundown that day, he was crucified at 9 a.m. and died at 3 p.m. Thursday. Because the Feast of Unleavened Bread, known as a high Sabbath or Shabbaton (a holy day where no work was to be done), they had to get Jesus' body off the cross before the day changed at sundown. Hebrew festivals fall on different days of the week every year. When a feast begins on a day other than the weekly Sabbath (Friday night), it is considered a Shabbaton.

Side Note: Jesus told His disciples,

> *"For as Jonah was three days and three nights in the belly of the great fish, so will the Son of Man be three days and three nights in the heart of the earth."*
>
> *Matt. 12:40*

Knowing that the weekly Sabbath and the high Sabbath of the Feast of Unleavened Bread are different helps explain how Jesus fulfilled this prophecy. If He was put in the tomb before sundown on the weekly Sabbath, (sundown Friday to sundown Saturday), then it would not line up with the three days and three nights that were prophesied in Matt. 12:40. If Jesus died on Thursday at 3p.m. and was taken down before it turned to Friday, the Feast of Unleavened Bread Sabbath, then He would be in the tomb three nights and be raised the morning of the third day, which would have been Sunday morning. It explains the discrepancy of only two nights if Jesus was removed from the cross on Friday of the weekly Sabbath. This is yet another example of how important it is for us to understand the Jewish roots of our faith. How amazing that

Jesus was put in the tomb during the Feast of Unleavened Bread; the same feast that commemorates the children of Israel crossing the Red Sea and watching their enemies be destroyed and disarmed in those burial waters. *Colossians 2:14-15* says,

> *"...having wiped out the handwriting of requirements that was against us, which was contrary to us. And He has taken it out of the way, having nailed it to the cross. Having disarmed principalities and powers, He made a public spectacle of them, triumphing over them in it."*

It is also important to note how Jesus fulfilled the command in Exodus 12:4, not to break any of the Passover lamb's bones:

> *"Therefore, because it was the Preparation Day, that the bodies should not remain on the cross on the Sabbath (for that Sabbath was a high day), the Jews asked Pilate that their legs might be broken, and that they might be taken away. Then the soldiers came and broke the legs of the first and of the other who was crucified with Him. But when they came to Jesus and saw that He was already dead, they did not break His legs. But one of the soldiers pierced His side with a spear, and immediately blood and water came out. And he who has seen has testified, and his testimony is true; and he*

knows that he is telling the truth, so that you may believe. For these things were done that the Scripture should be fulfilled, "Not one of His bones shall be broken."
John 19:31-37

Jesus' body was wrapped in linen.

"Then he bought fine linen, took Him down, and wrapped Him in the linen. And he laid Him in a tomb which had been hewn out of the rock, and rolled a stone against the door of the tomb."
Mark 15:46

When the children of Israel left Egypt in the middle of the night, their first stop was to get Joseph's bones (Ex. 13:19). It is interesting that the place they take Jesus' body is also to a tomb of a man named Joseph. It was prophesied that Jesus, the Messiah, would be buried in the tomb of the rich (Is. 53:9; Matt. 27:57; Luke 23:51). Why was Jesus placed in the tomb of Joseph of Arimathea? Arimathea was another name for Ramah, where Samuel dwelt. It is five miles north of Jerusalem. This place is still called Ramah today. In ancient times, it was customary for Jews to be buried in Jerusalem. In fact, this practice is still done today because it is a traditional belief in Judaism that the resurrection of the dead will take place in Jerusalem first.

In the Book of Genesis Joseph, the son of Jacob, made the children of Israel take a vow that when they went to the Promised Land they would carry his bones with them (Gen.50:24-26). Ramah was a term that represented idolatry. Two countries were called the seat of idolatry in the ancient world: Babylon and Egypt. Joseph, the son of Jacob, was also known as Joseph of Ramah. Moses took the bones of Joseph with him when he and the children of Israel journeyed to Succoth (Ex. 13:19-20). Therefore, Joseph's tomb in Egypt was empty. The empty tomb of Joseph of Arimathea (Ramah), which stood for wickedness, was a fulfillment of Isaiah 53:9.

Jesus Became the Passover "Afikoman"

Remember the revelation I had during this ceremony at my in-laws house at my first Passover Seder? Soon after the Seder (order of service) begins, three matzahs are removed from a special bag and the middle one is broken, wrapped in a white linen napkin and hidden for the children to find at the end of the meal. The Holy Spirit revealed to me that it was clearly speaking of Jesus being broken, wrapped in a white burial shroud and buried in the tomb. The word "afikoman" came from the time of Jesus and was a Greek word that translates, "that which comes last". Because it was the last thing eaten at the Passover meal, it was also known as "the satisfaction", or the most satisfying part of the evening that lingers even when it is over.

"I am the living bread which came down from heaven. If anyone eats of this bread, he will live forever; and the bread that I shall give is My flesh, which I shall give for the life of the world."

John 6:51

"Therefore purge out the old leaven, that you may be a new lump, since you truly are unleavened. For indeed Christ, our Passover, was sacrificed for us. ⁸ Therefore let us keep the feast, not with old leaven, nor with the leaven of malice and wickedness, but with the unleavened bread of sincerity and truth."

1 Cor. 5:7-8

17ᵗʰ of Aviv: 1500 BC

First Fruits of Barley Harvest

"Speak to the children of Israel, and say to them: 'When you come into the land which I give to you, and reap its harvest, then you shall bring a sheaf of the firstfruits of your harvest to the priest. He shall wave the sheaf before the LORD, to be accepted on your behalf; on the day after the Sabbath the priest shall wave it."

Lev. 23:10-11

If you follow along in the book of Exodus, Moses only asked Pharaoh to let them go on a three-day journey to serve the Lord. After the death of the first born, Pharaoh told Moses to take the children of Israel out of Egypt like Moses had requested, (Ex. 12:31) a three-day journey. They left Egypt sometime between midnight and dawn on the 15th of Aviv, and the first place they went was to get Joseph's bones in Sukkot (Ex. 13:19-20). They camp there for the night (Num. 33:5), and in the morning, still the 15th of Aviv, they travel to Etham (Num 33:6), where they camp the night when the day changes to the 16th at sundown. The following morning, still the 16th, they journey to Pi Hahiroth next to the Red Sea (Num. 33:7). As it turns to the 17th at sundown, Pharaoh and his armies approach their camp. We see that Pharaoh did come on the evening of the 17th from Ex.14:20-21, and the Lord put a pillar of cloud and fire between their armies and the children of Israel. It says all that night (still the 17th from sundown to sundown), God's people crossed the Red Sea, and it says in Ex.14:23-24, that Pharaoh entered the Red Sea during the morning watch and God drowns them in the waters.

Side Note: The morning watch on a Jewish day is the last third of the night before dawn.

We know that the children of Israel come up on dry land out of the sea before sunrise on Aviv 17. This would later be written down in Lev. 23:10-11 as the Festival of the Firstfruits when barley, the first crop of the spring, is harvested. Later in the book of Hosea, God remembers these events and tenderly says, *"When Israel was a child, I loved him, And out of Egypt I called My son." (Hosea 11:1).* It is interesting to note that the same is said of Jesus in *Matt. 2:14-15*.

> *out of Egypt I called My son*

"When he arose, he took the young Child and His mother by night and departed for Egypt, and was there until the death of Herod, that it might be fulfilled which was spoken by the Lord through the prophet, saying, "Out of Egypt I called My Son."

17ᵗʰ of Aviv: 1500 years later

"Now on the first day of the week Mary Magdalene went to the tomb early, while it was still dark, and saw that the stone had been taken away from the tomb. Then she ran and came to Simon Peter, and to the other disciple, whom Jesus loved, and said to them, "They have taken the Lord out of the tomb, and we do not know where they have laid Him."

John 20:1-2

In the temple in Jerusalem on this day, the High priest would cut a sheaf of barley to be waved before God to keep this feast according to Moses' instructions in Leviticus:

"Speak to the children of Israel, and say to them: 'When you come into the land which I give to you, and reap its harvest, then you shall bring a sheaf of the firstfruits of your harvest to the priest. He

shall wave the sheaf before the LORD, to be accepted on your behalf; on the day after the Sabbath (the weekly Sabbath) the priest shall wave it."
Lev. 23:10-11, parenthesis added

In other words, on the Sunday after Passover, the barley sheaf was to be waved. This was the festival called the Firstfruits of the Barley Harvest. Keeping with the ceremonial custom of this feast, the priest in the temple ascended the steps to the altar and said, "Don't touch me, I have not yet ascended".

With that in mind, we are now able to understand the confusing thing Jesus spoke to Mary, his valued friend. After He had been raised from the dead and appeared to her, I am sure the first thing she wanted to do was run and give Jesus a joy filled hug. Jesus' comment to her seems like a harsh rebuke if the context is not understood.

"Jesus said to her, "Do not cling to Me, for I have not yet ascended to My Father; but go to My brethren and say to them, 'I am ascending to My Father and your Father, and to My God and your God.'"
John 20:17

As both the Suffering Servant and the Great High Priest, Jesus was fulfilling the next festival on the Leviticus 23 pattern. He had become the Passover Lamb, had been put in the tomb on the Feast of Unleavened Bread, and now He was fulfilling the Firstfruits of the Barley Harvest on Aviv 17, ascending to heaven as the wave offering before the Father! It is astounding in its perfection and yet

Jesus has one more former rain feast to fulfill as suffering Servant: the Feast of Shavuot (Feast of Weeks, or firstfruits of the wheat harvest).

So far I have found three significant biblical events that line up with Aviv 17, the feast of Firstfruits of the Barley Harvest. (Knowing God and the perfection of His word, I am sure there are more to be revealed!)

- ***Gen. 8:4: "Then the ark rested in the seventh month, the seventeenth day of the month, on the mountains of Ararat."*** Remember, before Exodus 12, the first month was Tishri, making the 7th month Aviv. This was Aviv 17th

- The children of Israel crossed the Red Sea all night on the 17th of Aviv and the morning of the 17th were raised on dry ground, Ex. 14:28-29.

- Jesus was in the grave from the end of the 14th of Aviv and the morning of the 17th of Aviv, He was raised from the dead and ascended to the Father as the Firstfruits of the barley harvest wave offering, and then appeared that evening to eat a meal with His disciples.

Side Note: According to the Talmud, the Passover lamb in Exodus was killed at 3p.m. on a Thursday Aviv 14; roasted and eaten at sundown turning to Friday, Aviv 15 and they left Egypt in the middle of the night. They arrived at the Red Sea on a Saturday Aviv 16; and at sundown, turning to Sunday, Aviv 17, they crossed all night arriving on the other side in the morning, still Sunday. The likelihood of even the days of the week lining up 1500 years later is nothing short of miraculous!!!

131

I love the fact that after Jesus ascended as the barley wave offering before the Father, He came back down to earth and appeared to two hopeless followers who were in despair over His death. They are walking down a road, discussing the tragedy of His crucifixion and the utter humility of His death. They grew up reading the scriptures about the suffering servant Messiah known as messiah ben Joseph, but their theology was fixed on the second concept of the Messiah, messiah ben David, the conquering King. Their minds and emotions were sad and confused and probably felt betrayed by Jesus Who was not the conqueror they had expected Him to be. They had put all their hope in a defeated, dead man on a cross and their faith was shaken. Jesus comes alongside them and asks one of those tender questions that He already knows the answer to.

"Then the one whose name was Cleopas answered and said to Him, "Are You the only stranger in Jerusalem, and have You not known the things which happened there in these days?" And He said to them, "What things?" So they said to Him, "The things concerning Jesus of Nazareth, who was a Prophet mighty in deed and word before God and all the people... But we were hoping that it was He who was going to redeem Israel. Indeed, besides all this, today is the third day since these things happened. Yes, and certain women of our company, who arrived at the tomb early, astonished us. When they did not find His body, they came saying that they had also seen a

132

*vision of angels who said He was alive.
And certain of those who were with us
went to the tomb and found it just as the
women had said; but Him they did not
see." Then He said to them, "O foolish
ones, and slow of heart to believe in all
that the prophets have spoken! Ought not
the Christ to have suffered these things
and to enter into His glory? (in other
words, "did you forget all the clues I tried
to give you about having to first come as
suffering Servant?")*

Luke 24:18-26

6ᵗʰ of Sivan: 1500 BC

Feast of Weeks, Shavuot

The last spring feast was Feast of Weeks or Shavuot,
meaning "weeks" in Hebrew. It was also known in Greek
as Pentecost (meaning 50). Once they cross the Red Sea it
was 7 weeks equaling 49 days plus the day of Firstfruits for
a total of 50 days before they reach the mountain in Ex. 19.
Again, let's look at the pattern that Moses walked the
children of Israel through in Exodus and then look at how
Jesus perfectly fulfilled this exact pattern 1500 years later:

*"'And you shall count for yourselves from
the day after the Sabbath, from the day
that you brought the sheaf of the wave*

133

offering: seven Sabbaths shall be completed. Count fifty days to the day after the seventh Sabbath; then you shall offer a new grain offering to the LORD."
Lev. 23:15-16

From this scripture in Ex. 23:15-16 we see that including the day of Firstfruits of the Barley Harvest, Aviv17, they were to count seven Sabbaths. Firstfruits is one day, plus seven weeks or forty-nine days = 50 days. Remember, Moses was taking them on a journey that started in Egypt and ends at Mt. Sinai. (Ex.12-19). The arrival to this mountain in Ex. 19 was the first Feast of Weeks or Shavuot and is remembered as the day God entered into a covenant partnership with the children of Israel.

If you count according to what was written in Leviticus 23: 15-16, the Feast of Weeks or Shavuot, falls on the third Hebrew month of Sivan. Moses led the children of Israel on a fifty-day journey to bring the Children of Israel to Mt. Sinai to enter into a marriage covenant with God. The LORD had fed them with supernatural food and given them water from a rock. He was their cloud by day to protect them from the sun and their fire by night to keep them warm. He was El Shaddai, their provider, showing them His goodness and kindness towards His people. He was changing their identity through their journey from slaves to sons and then to priests; but ultimately, God's purpose in bringing them out of Egypt was to be His Bride. Exodus 19 gives the account of Moses bringing the people to the mountain to hear God's voice. The trumpet sounded to summons the Bride and then Moses went up to receive God's words. God manifests His awesome and terrifying presence on this first Feast of Weeks in the following verses:

"In the third month after the children of Israel had gone out of the land of Egypt, on the same day, they came to the Wilderness of Sinai. For they had departed from Rephidim, had come to the Wilderness of Sinai, and camped in the wilderness. So Israel camped there before the mountain. And Moses went up to God, and the LORD called to him from the mountain, saying, "Thus you shall say to the house of Jacob, and tell the children of Israel: 'You have seen what I did to the Egyptians, and how I bore you on eagles' wings and brought you to Myself. Now therefore, if you will indeed obey My voice and keep My covenant, then you shall be a special treasure to Me above all people; for all the earth is Mine. And you shall be to Me a kingdom of priests and a holy nation.' These are the words which you shall speak to the children of Israel." So Moses came and called for the elders of the people, and laid before them all these words which the LORD commanded him. Then all the people answered together and said, "All that the LORD has spoken we will do." So Moses brought back the words of the people to the LORD. And the LORD said to Moses, "Behold, I come to you in the thick cloud, that the people

may hear when I speak with you, and believe you forever." So Moses told the words of the people to the LORD... Then it came to pass on the third day, in the morning, that there were thunderings and lightnings, and a thick cloud on the mountain; and the sound of the trumpet was very loud, so that all the people who were in the camp trembled. And Moses brought the people out of the camp to meet with God, and they stood at the foot of the mountain. Now Mount Sinai was completely in smoke, because the LORD descended upon it in fire. Its smoke ascended like the smoke of a furnace, and the whole mountain quaked greatly. And when the blast of the trumpet sounded long and became louder and louder, Moses spoke, and God answered him by voice. Then the LORD came down upon Mount Sinai, on the top of the mountain. And the LORD called Moses to the top of the mountain, and Moses went up."

> *Then the LORD came down...and Moses went up*

Ex. 19:1-9, 16-20

It was at this time that the children of Israel agreed to receive God to be their only God and to keep the covenant that was given to Moses. We will see that 1500 years later, in Acts 2, this same feast was fulfilled by Jesus. He gave a gift to His bride that was more than words on tablets of stone but sealed His word in their hearts with the outpouring of His Spirit within them.

6th of Sivan: 1500 years later

Jesus tells His disciples that there is one more appointment that He is going to keep with them, one more spring moed to fulfill. He tells them to go to Jerusalem and wait for Him to keep it.

> *"Then He said to them, "These are the words which I spoke to you while I was still with you, that all things must be fulfilled which were written in the Law of Moses and the Prophets and the Psalms concerning Me." And He opened their understanding, that they might comprehend the Scriptures. Then He said to them, "Thus it is written, and thus it was necessary for the Christ to suffer and to rise from the dead the third day, and that repentance and remission of sins should be preached in His name to all nations, beginning at Jerusalem. And you are witnesses of these things. Behold, I send the Promise of My Father upon you; but tarry in the city of Jerusalem until you are endued with power from on high."*
>
> *Luke 24:44-49*

And what is the day they are waiting for that He will fulfill? The answer is in the first verse of **Acts 2:1**.

> *"When the Day of Pentecost had fully come, they were all with one accord in one place. And suddenly there came a sound from heaven, as of a rushing mighty wind, and it filled the whole house where they were sitting. Then there appeared to them divided tongues, as of fire, and one sat upon each of them. And they were all filled with the Holy Spirit and began to speak with other tongues, as the Spirit gave them utterance."*

What does it mean that when the day of Pentecost had fully come? It means when He has fully kept the appointment that has been on His appointment book from the beginning of time and was written down in Leviticus 23!

Now please read in **Appendix H** the excerpt from the Talmud of the account of the first Shavuot on Mt. Sinai that was recorded in Jewish history. It is phenomenal because Jewish historians that do not believe in Jesus or the New Testament wrote it! Trust me, they do not want it to line up with the account in Acts 2!

> *Trust me, they do not want it to line up with the account in Acts 2!*

Conclusion

Years ago, when I first discovered how perfectly Jesus walked through the pattern of the spring feasts, I was astounded! The fact that 1500 years before the time of

Jesus, God set in motion His plan of redemption. First He had Moses walk through it, leading the children of Israel out of Egypt in order to take them to a mountain to be His covenant partner. Then He made sure Moses wrote it down in Leviticus 23 so these set times on His calendar, that spoke of His appointed times He would come to earth, would be kept alive from generation to generation. If what you just read in this chapter has not hit you yet, pray for a spirit of revelation until it does! God has an appointment book. It is Leviticus 23. He has shown up to His first four appointments. He will surely be as faithful to the remaining three; unless He has lost the appointment book, which is not likely.

First Moses, then Jesus... only God could unfold and write such a brilliant story! Even though we can only see a glimpse or shadow of what's coming, it is exciting to be living in a time when He wants to reveal Himself in our biblical roots. I want to give you a holy expectation to pray that as you begin this journey to find Jesus in the feasts, He will open your eyes to see the glory and the mysteries that are nuggets of gold waiting for you to stumble into, pick up and fall in love with Him again and again.

Moses in the Tent of Meeting

I chose the picture on the cover of this book that my friend drew years ago, because to me, this is where the story begins and ends. God appeared to Moses in a burning bush and told Him His name. Then He gave Moses an assignment to deliver His people out of Egypt and take them to a mountain to enter into a covenant partnership. The people knew God from afar. They saw His power and might and trembled at His presence. They knew "about" God but never drew near in a desire to know Him intimately for themselves. Moses didn't only stop to marvel at a bush on fire but wanted to know the one speaking to Him for himself. He was not afraid to ask Him questions about Who He was, and was personal enough to dare argue with God over his inadequacies to complete the task he was being called to. God was his friend and they had a heart to heart, real relationship. He went up Mt. Sinai and God came down and revealed His glory to Moses. But it was in a small tent of meeting when Moses was in anguish over the future of his people that scripture records an astounding fact. ***"So the LORD spoke to Moses face to face, as a man speaks to his friend." (Ex. 33:11)*** This is what God is yearning for from His people. This is why He was willing to come to earth and set in motion His brilliant plan to redeem His bride. This desire to have an intimate, face-to-face relationship… a partnership that

Moses found the Afikoman	would bring light and healing and restoration to the whole earth and to all nations… THIS was the joy set before Him. When Moses entered into that little tent of meeting in the wilderness, He found the pearl of great price,

the one thing that alone can satisfy. Moses found the Afikoman.

"You are faithful to the end,
Faithful to my heart.
Faithful to the end,
You will come and marry me"

Melissa Mahoney

~ Chapter 5 ~

Passover and the Four Cups of Redemption

"Therefore say to the children of Israel: 'I am the LORD; I will bring you out from under the burdens of the Egyptians, I will rescue you from their bondage, and I will redeem you with an outstretched arm and with great judgments. I will take you as My people, and I will be your God. Then you shall know that I am the LORD your God who brings you out from under the burdens of the Egyptians."
Ex. 6:6-7

Before I begin telling you how I discovered God's heart in the four cups of redemption found within the liturgy of a Passover Seder, I will briefly explain what a Seder is in case there are some who have never participated in one. Seder means, "order", as in the order of a service. So as the order of the evening unfolds, all the participants are part of a play that is rehearsed yearly to remember what God has done for them. The way the Feast has been kept yearly for thousands of years is to tell the story of the exodus out of Egypt at the family Seder table. The table is beautifully set with a white linen tablecloth, fine china, candles, flowers and all the elements needed to walk through the story of the journey out of bondage to freedom. Hebrew learning is with the senses. Consequently, each step of deliverance is experienced, not only by telling the story, but also by eating special foods symbolic of their bondage, and drinking four cups of wine throughout the evening. Wine is used

> *all the participants are part of a play that is rehearsed yearly to remember what God has done for them*

because it represents the joy of the Holy Spirit that increases as the Seder progresses so that by the end of the evening, freedom is felt! The "script" for the evening is called a haggadah and each person at the table walks through the steps of their own deliverance as though they were there.

Years ago, when I first started searching for Jesus in the feasts, I was focused on finding His heart in the Passover Seder celebration. I could see the types and shadows in the book of Exodus and how they were meaningful to Christians as well as to Jews. I could see that just as the children of Israel were captive slaves to Pharaoh in the land of Egypt in the natural, so too are we as Christians in captivity to a world system under Satan before we are born again. Likewise, just as the way out for the Israelites under the leadership of Moses, their deliverer, was by the blood of a lamb on the doorposts of their homes; so is our deliverance achieved by the blood of Jesus, the Lamb of God, applied to our lives. Even on this symbolic level, participating in a traditional Passover Seder can be very interesting for every born again Christian to experience; but

I knew in my heart that I wanted more, and I asked the Holy Spirit to show me where His heart was and how we could encounter Jesus in the Passover. He was the Passover Afikoman, "the satisfaction", and I was not satisfied with types and shadows alone. So year after year we would go through the Passover ceremony, and as we did, I would pray for understanding and encounter.

A few years into seeking Him for revelation, I was at a Jewish gift store near my mother-in-law's house and a greeting card on a display caught my eye. On the front of this particular Passover greeting card were four large cups of wine. I felt the Lord say, "This is where you will find My heart... look for Me in the four cups of redemption". I quickly bought the card and left, excited that He had finally spoken to me. I felt like a child getting the first clue to a treasure hunt!

I had read Jewish books about the holidays and I knew that Jewish people were mandated to drink four cups of wine throughout the Passover Seder. Because it was referred to as "the festival of freedom", they are commanded to use wine so they can literally feel free by the end of the evening! As one rabbi commented when asked

> *Hebrew learning is experiential*

why it had to be wine and not grape juice, he replied with the obvious; "Because it is impossible to drink grape juice and keep the mandate to feel free at the end of the evening!"

Hebrew learning is experiential. Young children are given honey to eat when they begin studying the Torah (the first 5 books of the Bible) to remind them that the Word is sweet. When you experience learning with your senses as well as your mind, your heart remembers.

1 John 1:1 says,

> *"That which was from the beginning, which we have heard, which we have seen with our eyes, which we have looked upon, and our hands have handled, of the Word of life-".*

He is to be experienced, and somehow in my heart I knew I had found the focal point of encountering Jesus in a Passover. At the Seders I've been a part of very little is said about the richness of these four cups. They are named according to the four "I wills" found in *Exodus 6:6-7*.

> *"Therefore say to the children of Israel: 'I am the LORD; I will bring you out from under the burdens of the Egyptians, I will rescue you from their bondage, and I will redeem you with an outstretched arm and with great judgments. I will take you as My people, and I will be your God. Then you shall know that I am the LORD your God who brings you out from under the burdens of the Egyptians."*

Cups of Redemption

• The first cup, or the first "I will" •

"…I will bring you out of the burden of the
Egyptians…"
Ex:6:6

When I was meditating on this verse, asking Him to
open it up to me, I came across an interesting commentary
in a Jewish haggadah. Remember, a haggadah is the
booklet, or "script" that Jewish people use to go through
the liturgy of the Passover Seder ceremony. I said in an
earlier chapter that the festivals are His "moedim",
appointments on His appointment book, and they are to be
"rehearsed" every year. For this reason, every Passover is
the reenactment of the exodus from Egypt that Jews are to
keep forever.

> *"…You shall keep it as a feast by an*
> *everlasting ordinance."*
>
> *Ex. 12:14*

God says over and over throughout the Bible to,
"Remember, I am the God of Abraham, Isaac, and Jacob Who
delivered you from bondage to the Egyptians with a mighty
outstretched arm", and in observing year after year, generation
to generation, they never forget. So the Passover is an
evening of participation. No one is a passive bystander.
During the evening you drink four cups of wine and eat
symbolic foods like bitter herbs and horseradish to
symbolize the bitterness of slavery. Likewise you are to eat
flat matzahs, unleavened bread, the bread of affliction, to

145

remind you that when God came down to deliver His people, they could not tarry or be indecisive…they had to leave in haste with no time for their bread to rise. All these things are in the haggadah to partake of in the proper order as we rehearse the steps of our deliverance.

So, with that brief explanation of a haggadah, I want to share an interesting commentary on the first cup from Rabbi Abraham Twerski in his hagadah called, From Bondage to Freedom. Rabbi Twerski says,

> "In commissioning Moses to liberate the Israelites from Egypt, God said, 'I will extract them from the burden (sivlus) of Egypt' (Ex 6:6). Rabbi Isaac Meir points out that the word "sivus" also means "tolerance," and the sentence then reads, 'I will extract them from the tolerance of Egypt.' During the many years of enslavement, the Israelites had become so accustomed to their status that they considered it to be a normal state of affairs. Not only had they resigned themselves to being slaves, but also had come to believe that this was their natural state, much like the proverbial worm who infests the horseradish and undoubtedly considers this, the bitterest of all vegetables, to be the best place in the world… without Divine intervention we would not have extricated ourselves from Egypt, because we had no aspiration for liberty… The story of the Exodus should serve as an arousal to every individual. It

should alert one to think, 'Is it possible that I may be in a rut, but similar to my enslaved ancestors not recognize it? This should stimulate one to rigorous self-examination, and to a determination that if there is indeed a more worthy lifestyle, one should be willing to bear the temporary discomfort in making the necessary changes in one's life to achieve the true liberty that dignifies a human being."

pp. 67-68

All of a sudden, I felt the Lord was revealing something to me about how to experience that first cup of redemption. God had a problem. It was His appointed time on His calendar to "come down" and deliver them, but after 430 years of slavery, their bondage was so familiar to them that they had lost any desire for freedom. He would come down when He heard them cry, but first they had to cry out. This is the first step that God supernaturally initiates to redeem His people. He makes them hate their bondage... He makes them lose their toleration to being slaves and creates a sudden corporate cry for Him to set them free! We see this miraculous event in Exodus.

"And the Lord said: "I have surely seen the oppression of My people who are in Egypt, and have heard their cry because of their taskmasters, for I know their sorrows. So I have come down (yarad) to deliver them out of the hand of the Egyptians, and to bring them up from that

land to a good and a large land, to a land flowing with milk and honey, to the place of the Canaanites and the Hittites and the Amorites and the Perizzites and the Hivites and the Jebusites. Now therefore, behold, the cry of the children of Israel has come to Me, and I have also seen the oppression with which the Egyptians oppress them. Come now, therefore, and I will send you to Pharaoh that you may bring forth My people, the children of Israel, out of Egypt."

Ex. 3:7-10

Side Note: You should consider doing a word study on the Hebrew word "yarad", meaning, when God "comes down". You will find that it is only seen on very special and dramatic occasions as evidenced in Genesis 11 when God comes down to deal with the building of the Tower of Babel. It is in other significant places and I just wanted to draw your attention to it.

After finding this commentary on the first cup meaning delivering the children of Israel from the tolerance to their bondage, God began to open my eyes to the meaning behind this important first step of deliverance so we, as born again believers, could encounter Him in it. Over the years of doing many Passover Seders, most of the people present at our table are people that are already born again believers. Because of this, we are usually not asking for deliverance out of the world (Egypt), and deliverance from Satan's (Pharaoh) ownership of us. But we do pause before partaking of this cup together to remember the miraculous details of how we were lost and He revealed Himself to us and supernaturally saved us. It would be good to remember this often, but Passover provides a time to stop, contemplate, and be thankful for what God so mercifully did for us. However, salvation is not just referring to what God has done in the past but what He is present to do throughout our lifetime.

We are all in need of salvation continually. We all tolerate things in our lives that are so familiar to us that, like the children of Israel, we have no aspiration for freedom because either we do not even see our bondage, or if we do, we say, "it's not that bad. I can live with it." God does not want us to tolerate anything that keeps us from loving Him fully, loving others fully, or that keeps us in bondage to the enemy in any way. He is coming for a pure and spotless bride and He wants us free. The first cup of redemption is an opportunity yearly to sit before the Lord and ask Him to make us hate any bondage in our lives and to expose anything we are tolerating that is keeping us oppressed or bound. He will do it and He will produce the cry in us to be free so He can answer.

> *He will produce the cry in us to be free so He can answer.*

There is a good example of this found in 1 Samuel 1. We see the story of Hannah who is in distress because her husband had another wife who could have children but Hannah was barren. It said that year after year this other wife provoked Hannah to the point of despair so much so that she could not even eat. But one year, I believe at the appointed time for Samuel to be born, Hannah's anguished cry went up before the Lord and she was

> *God produced a cry in her that moved heaven*

delivered from her barrenness and Samuel was conceived. What changed after many years of torment and grief of her barrenness? God produced a cry in her that moved heaven.

Every year at Passover, the first cup of redemption is an opportunity for us to ask God to reveal habits, attitudes, bondages, sickness, or any other things that we are tolerating that steals life from us in any way. It is a powerful prayer and each year we can have an expectation that God will answer when He hears our cry. It is also a powerful prayer if you know someone bound by sin or addiction to pray that God would take away their toleration of it and they would suddenly hate it, see it as an enemy, and cry out for freedom.

This first cup is powerful. It begins with God's initiative to supernaturally draw those that are called to be His, by creating a cry for freedom and a desire for Him to show up in our circumstances and come down for us personally. The children of Israel had heard stories of a God Who had appeared to their forefathers but now they needed to know Him for themselves. There is something about the familiar prayer, "God if you are real, show me and answer," that gets results when it is sincere. In some form or another, it is how all of us first got saved. So we pray for that first cup of redemption found in ***Exodus 6:6, "…I will bring you out from under the burdens (toleration) of the Egyptians."*** We pray, we wait on the Lord, and offer our silent, individual prayers up to a merciful and faithful God to do His part and answer our cry for deliverance.

• The second cup, or second "I will" •

"I will rescue you from their bondage..."
(Ex. 6:6)

After being slaves for 400 years, the children of Israel had no aspiration for freedom. In the first cup of redemption we saw how God had to supernaturally make them hate their bondage and remove their tolerance to it, so they would cry out to Him. He was faithful to answer.

> *"And the LORD said: "I have surely seen the oppression of My people who are in Egypt, and have heard their cry because of their taskmasters, for I know their sorrows. So I have come down to deliver them out of the hand of the Egyptians..."*
> *Ex.3:7-8*

This cup of redemption during the Passover is incredibly significant for us as believers in Jesus, and I feel that there is a holy moment to wait on Him as individuals before we partake of it together. God had waited 430 years while Jacob's family became a great multitude in Egypt. But their sojourning in this land was not permanent. He promised Abraham,

> *"...Know certainly that your descendants will be strangers in a land that is not theirs, and will serve them, and they will afflict them four hundred years."*
> *Gen. 15:13*

Also, later on, in the same chapter, God promised Abraham that his descendants would inherit a land of their own.

The time has come for God to keep an appointment. He has stood by and watched His people whom He loves, being oppressed and abused and held captive by an evil ruler for hundreds of years. Now He has heard their cry for Him to answer and He is ready to come down. I feel the soberness of the moment; a fear of the Lord kind of moment that takes your breath away. I am remembering a poster I saw of the movie, "Braveheart", with Mel Gibson. His bride has just been killed and he has the fury of a grieving bridegroom on his face. He has his army arrayed with their weapons poised, waiting for the signal for the battle to begin. Mel Gibson is sitting on his horse with war paint on his face and fire in his eyes. All you can think is, "Woe to the enemy". The caption reads, "It's time."

> *The time has come for God to keep an appointment*

Now it is time for God to free His people and bring devastation and judgment to the nation that held them in bondage. God gives Moses specific directions. He is coming down to get them out of Egypt but this is no time for lawlessness or disobedience. He will do His part but they must have faith in Him and obey. All who want to be delivered have to participate. The instructions are given in Exodus.

> **"Speak to all the congregation of Israel, saying: 'On the tenth of this month every man shall take for himself a lamb, according to the house of his father, a lamb for a household. And if the**

152

household is too small for the lamb, let him and his neighbor next to his house take it according to the number of the persons; according to each man's need you shall make your count for the lamb. Your lamb shall be without blemish, a male of the first year. You may take it from the sheep or from the goats. Now you shall keep it until the fourteenth day of the same month. Then the whole assembly of the congregation of Israel shall kill it at twilight. And they shall take some of the blood and put it on the two doorposts and on the lintel of the houses where they eat it. Then they shall eat the flesh on that night; roasted in fire, with unleavened bread and with bitter herbs they shall eat it. Do not eat it raw, nor boiled at all with water, but roasted in fire—its head with its legs and its entrails. You shall let none of it remain until morning, and what remains of it until morning you shall burn with fire. And thus you shall eat it: with a belt on your waist, your sandals on your feet, and your staff in your hand. So you shall eat it in haste. It is the LORD's Passover. 'For I will pass through the land of Egypt on that night, and will strike all the firstborn in the land of Egypt, both man and beast; and against all the gods of Egypt I will execute judgment: I am the LORD. Now the blood shall be a sign for you on the

houses where you are. And when I see the
blood, I will pass over you; and the plague
shall not be on you to destroy you when I
strike the land of Egypt."
                                              Ex. 12:3-13

There was one way out of Egypt. It was by placing the
blood of the sacrificed lamb on the doorposts of your
dwelling. There is one way out of the world where we are
held legally captive to Satan's domain of darkness. It is by
the blood of Jesus applied to our lives.

"Knowing that you were not redeemed
with corruptible things, like silver or gold,
from your aimless conduct received by
tradition from your fathers, but with the
precious blood of Christ, as of a lamb
without blemish and without spot."
                                              1 Peter 1:18-19

Exodus 12:23 says,

"...when He sees the blood... the LORD
will pass over..."

In Exodus 12:12, He says He will pass through the land of
Egypt. The word "pass through" is the Hebrew word
"abar" or "gabar". When God passes through, it is to bring
judgment on His enemies. But, He will pass over when He
sees the blood on the doorposts. The Hebrew word for
passover is "pesach". I remember hearing a teaching that
the word "pesach" carries the same picture as in Psalm 91
of being covered or hidden under His protective wings in

an intimate place with Him. I wish I could find the commentary so I could reference it, but I wrote in my notes that the teacher said it means like a mother bird spreading her wings over her young to hide and protect them from predators. With that in mind, let's read the verses in Psalm 91:

> *"He who dwells in the secret place of the Most High Shall abide under the shadow of the Almighty. I will say of the LORD, "He is my refuge and my fortress; My God, in Him I will trust." Surely He shall deliver you from the snare of the fowler And from the perilous pestilence. He shall cover you with His feathers, And under His wings you shall take refuge; His truth shall be your shield and buckler. You shall not be afraid of the terror by night, Nor of the arrow that flies by day, Nor of the pestilence that walks in darkness, Nor of the destruction that lays waste at noonday."*
>
> *Ps. 91:1-6*

God even uses a similar, tender picture in Exodus 19, recounting the way He brought them out:

> *"And Moses went up to God, and the LORD called to him from the mountain, saying, "Thus you shall say to the house of Jacob, and tell the children of Israel:*

'You have seen what I did to the Egyptians, and how I bore you on eagles' wings and brought you to Myself."

Ex: 19:3-4

Also, in the story of Ruth and Boaz we see this same intimate imagery of protective wings being used:

"Now it happened at midnight that the man was startled, and turned himself; and there, a woman was lying at his feet. And he said, "Who are you?" So she answered, "I am Ruth, your maidservant. Take your maidservant under your wing, for you are a close relative."

Ruth 3:8-9

When we recall the Exodus story I think we often reduce it to the "family friendly" version instead of the "R" rating it actually deserves. Evil was being confronted and the spiritual realms of darkness that were major demonic strongholds were being stirred up and brought down. Every god of Egypt was humiliated and destroyed when the 10 plagues were released, including Pharoah himself. There was blood and pestilence, disease and death; the degree of human suffering was unimaginable. Egypt was being disrupted and destroyed in every way. God wanted His people as His "special treasure" (Ex. 19).

When Pharaoh stubbornly refused to let them go, God's zealous judgment was released against the nation. *Deuteronomy 26:8* says, *"So the LORD brought us out of Egypt with a mighty hand and with an outstretched arm, with great terror and with signs and wonders."*

While God is revealing Himself to His enemies as a strong warrior with a "mighty outstretched hand" of judgment, at the same time, to His people, who He is taking to a mountain to be His betrothed bride, he remembers it as ***"...the day when I took them by the hand to lead them out of the land of Egypt..." (Heb. 8:9)*** Again in ***Jeremiah 2:2,*** we hear the tender perspective of a Bridegroom delivering His bride:

> *"Go and cry in the hearing of Jerusalem, saying, 'Thus says the Lord: "I remember you, The kindness of your youth, The love of your betrothal, When you went after Me in the wilderness, In a land not sown."*

The second cup of redemption is powerful on many levels. The children of Israel are leaving in the middle of the night, they have plundered Egypt of their gold and silver, and they are leaving healed!

> *"He also brought them out with silver and gold, And there was none feeble among His tribes. Egypt was glad when they departed, For the fear of them had fallen upon them."*
>
> ***Ps. 105:37-38***

As we pause before taking this second cup of redemption we have much to think about. This time, every year, we have an opportunity to be with our friends and family and remember the powerful testimony of Jesus in our lives. I sit and remember how utterly lost and hopeless I was before He saved me. I remember how miraculous it was that He somehow put a yearning and hunger inside of me to know Him, and all the details and circumstances He had to set up in John and my life to get us to come find Him. He delivered me out of deep darkness and fear and brought me into the safety of His amazing love. But the main focus of this cup is to remember the cost of my deliverance;

> *"Knowing that you were not redeemed with corruptible things... but with the precious blood of Christ, as of a lamb without blemish and without spot."*
> *1 Peter 1:18-19*

Bob Sorge, one of my all-time favorite author's, wrote this in his book, <u>Power of the Blood</u>:

"When I can't make sense of my journey, I go back to the cross. When I can't process my pain levels, I go back to the cross. When my wound seems incurable, I go back to the cross. When I can't see my way forward, I go back to the cross. When I feel like He is withholding from me, I go back to the cross. Because sometimes the accuser hits me with that ancient accusation, 'God's withholding from you. He could deliver you right now, but He is holding out on you... But the cross nailed that accusation. Because when I look at the cross, I see a God with nails in His hands, a nail in His feet, a crown of thorns on His brow, and stripes on His back. As

He hangs there with His arms spread wide, He says to me, 'I give you My heart, I give you My body, I give you My all, I give you My last breath, I give you My last drop of blood.'

I declare to you that my God withholds nothing from me! He has given me His best. He has given me His all. His extravagance has empowered me, in turn, to withhold nothing from Him. He has given me His everything, and now I give Him my everything. I am His and He is mine.

God doesn't ever have to do another thing for me, to prove that He loves me. If He never does anything for me ever again---if He never blesses me, if He never answers my prayer, if He never delivers me--- the cross is enough to prove the authenticity of His undying affection. It's because of the cross that I know He loves me!

And since His cross has made me so confident in love, I will never be silent; I will never relent; I will never let go; but I will always lift my cry to God and call on His name; until He fulfills His promise and delivers me." (pp. 14-15)

So with awe and wonder and a heart overflowing with thankfulness and love for all this second cup represents to me I celebrate and drink with joy this second "I will" of Exodus 6:6 and rejoice that He proclaims His love to me by saying, "I will rescue you from their bondage." "L' Chaim! To Life!"

• Introduction to the third cup •

After thirty-nine years of doing Passover Seders in our home, I still get butterflies in my stomach and feel an intense excitement before our guests walk in the door. For days, I make my preparations getting everything ready, "setting the stage" with a holy expectation that God will come and encounter hearts. The main reason I love to celebrate the feasts with others is a selfish one. I love the preparation. I love putting on my white tablecloth, setting out my china and pink crystal wine glasses, seeing the prepared, individual seder plates in the middle of each large plate with the symbolic foods all ready to partake of. The flowers are placed in vases and the silver candlesticks are ready to be lit, in order to begin our evening "journey out of Egypt". Right before our guests arrive, I stand and see the beauty my eyes are beholding, and feel what an awesome privilege it is to be able to prepare a place for Him to come. I love it because He loves it, and in that moment, I feel the reward of feeling His presence and His pleasure.

what an awesome privilege it is to be able to prepare a place for Him to come

I also know, without a doubt, that God will faithfully come and lead his precious people, into whom He has invested His all, through the steps of our salvation. We will remember the day we felt His tender pull on our hearts, and He answered our cry by supernaturally delivering us from darkness into His Kingdom of light. We will remember how lost we were without Him, and the extravagant price He paid to redeem our souls. We will remember that we were once slaves to a cruel taskmaster (Satan), and the bitterness of our bondage before we were set free.

Sitting at our table, feasting with brothers and sisters, sharing in this journey together, feeling the progression of our freedom together as each cup of wine is drunk, and yet each one of us has our own unique story, our own prophetic history that we are reliving personally before the Lord. It is powerful to watch thankful hearts and tear streamed faces as we sit before the King of the universe, and with each cup, we remember. All throughout the Bible after the Exodus, God reminds them Who He is and says over and over again, ***"I am the God of Abraham, Isaac, and Jacob, Who delivered you out of Egypt by a mighty, outstretched arm"*** He does NOT want us to forget, so He reminds us and we remember, each year at the festival of Passover, the steps of our redemption.

I seriously enjoy the whole evening, but my very favorite moment comes when the meal has been eaten, plates are cleared, and we are ready to partake of the third cup. I feel my heart start pounding as I get the privilege to tell this part of His story, and reveal His astounding heart motive behind all that He has done for us.

• The third cup, or the third "I will" •

"...I will redeem you with an outstretched arm and
with great judgments."
Ex. 6:6

Redeem means, in Hebrew, "to buy back". We see this implied in many scriptures, but a few examples are:

"...the people... whom You have purchased"
Ex. 15:16

and,

"...Is He not your Father, who bought you?"
Deut. 32:6

And in the New Testament,

"For you were bought at a price..."
1 Cor. 6:20

"Knowing that you were not redeemed
with corruptible things, like silver or gold,
from your aimless conduct received by
tradition from your fathers, but with the
precious blood of Christ, as of a lamb
without blemish and without spot."
1 Peter 1:18-19

I mentioned in chapter two the concept of a redeemer, called in Hebrew, a "goel". A goel was known as a "kinsmen redeemer", each family/tribe had one. He would go to the enemy's camp, or to a person who had suffered a crime at the hand of another (or a misfortune, as in the story of Naomi in the Book of Ruth), and pay a redemption price to "buy back" the family member. The price is paid for them to be returned or restored to their land or to their family. In the Book of Ruth we see an example of the lineage of Naomi and Elimelek being redeemed through the marriage of Ruth and Boaz.

We saw in the second Passover cup, that the way out of Egypt was bought for the Israelites by the blood of a lamb on their doorposts. It paid their way out of Egypt (the world), and bought them healing of their bodies as they left (Ps. 105:37), but their freedom and redemption was not complete until they were brought to someone and someplace with a new identity. Just to be rid of a yoke of bondage under the possession of Pharaoh was not enough. To be totally free people, they had to come under the possession and Lordship of One Who could love them, care for them and protect them from their enemies.

Remember we said in the first cup that God had a problem? That a people that have been slaves for 430 years have no aspiration for freedom and He would only come down to rescue them when He heard their cry for freedom? Then we saw how God had to supernaturally make them hate their bondage and end their toleration to slavery. An anguished cry came forth and He came down to deliver them. His mighty arm of judgment had destroyed Egypt and brought them out with mighty signs and wonders, but now God faced His second problem. The Israelites were the legal possession of Pharaoh, and God does everything legally. In Genesis 47, everyone in Egypt, with the exception of Pharaoh's priests,

The Israelites were the legal possession of Pharaoh, and God does everything legally.

agreed to sell themselves to Pharaoh for bread during the time of famine:

> *"Then Joseph said to the people, "Indeed I have bought you and your land this day for Pharaoh. Look, here is seed for you, and you shall sow the land... So they said, "You have saved our lives; let us find favor in the sight of my lord, and we will be Pharaoh's servants."*
>
> *Gen. 47:23, 25*

Now, in this third step of redemption, God had to somehow transfer them legally from Pharaoh's ownership to His own and to transfer them from an evil kingdom of darkness into His Kingdom where they were no longer to be slaves, but His own special people. He tells them,

> *"'You have seen what I did to the Egyptians, and how I bore you on eagles' wings and brought you to Myself. Now therefore, if you will indeed obey My voice and keep My covenant, then you shall be a special treasure to Me above all people; for all the earth is Mine. And you shall be to Me a kingdom of priests and a holy nation.'..."*
>
> *Ex. 19:4-6*

How does God legally get them from the ownership of Pharaoh to be His own? The third cup of redemption gives us the answer. Remember, Moses only asked permission to take the children of Israel on a three-day journey into the wilderness to hold a feast unto the Lord. When Moses arrives with them at the shores of the Red Sea, at sundown it turns to the 3rd day. (Refer to chapter 4 and you will see this was sundown turning to the 17th of Aviv). It was here where the Israelites looked back, paralyzed with fear, to see Pharaoh and his army coming to take them back! God then has Moses lift his staff and say,

> *"…Do not be afraid. Stand still, and see the salvation of the LORD, which He will accomplish for you today. For the Egyptians whom you see today, you shall see again no more forever."*
>
> *Ex.14:13*

Then the miraculous happens; God dries up the great sea, and all night long, the children of Israel cross and on the morning of Aviv 17, they are raised up on the other side. They look back and see Pharaoh and his army drowned, floating on top of the water. A covenant, like marriage, is broken with the death of one "husband" making it legal to marry another (1 Cor. 7:39). We will see in the next chapter when I talk about the final 4th cup of redemption (called the cup of consummation), that God was taking them to a mountain for marriage. With their old covenant now broken by death, they were now free to become His covenant people.

How does this pattern relate to us as New Testament believers in Jesus? It is incredibly important for us to understand what happened in those waters because this pattern of their redemption and deliverance was given to us as well as to them. The children of Israel had come out of Egypt but now they needed to get the defilement of

Egypt off of them and become clean so they could take on a new identity before appearing on the mountain to meet with God. When they passed through those waters, it was a type of baptism, burying the old man so they could be raised a new creation on the other side. It was the waters, after they had crossed, that separated them from their former life of bondage. Egypt was no longer able to pursue them to try to take them back to their old identity as slaves. They could look back, and see their enemies disarmed and their bodies floating on the waters. ***Colossians 2:12-15*** says:

> *"buried with Him in baptism, in which you also were raised with Him through faith in the working of God, who raised Him from the dead... Having disarmed principalities and powers, He made a public spectacle of them, triumphing over them in it."*

Wow! Do you see it? Now look at this next verse:

> *"For Christ also suffered once for sins, the just for the unjust, that He might bring us to God, being put to death in the flesh but made alive by the Spirit, by whom also He went and preached to the spirits in prison, who formerly were disobedient, when once the Divine longsuffering waited in the days of Noah, while the ark was being prepared, in which a few, that is, eight souls, were saved through water. There is also an antitype, which now saves us—*

baptism (not the removal of the filth of the flesh, but the answer of a good conscience toward God), through the resurrection of Jesus Christ, who has gone into heaven and is at the right hand of God, angels and authorities and powers having been made subject to Him."

1 Peter 3:18-22

"He who believes and is baptized will be saved; but he who does not believe will be condemned."

Mark 16:16

I used to read those scriptures and get confused. They seem to say baptism saves us, and whole denominations hang their theology on this verse. But I do not believe Peter is talking about salvation from Hell. We know it is the blood of Jesus applied to our lives that saves us out of Hell. But there are principalities, powers and demonic strongholds that we partake of and come into agreement with before we are saved. These are what God cuts off from us when we enter the waters of baptism.

"Therefore we were buried with Him through baptism into death, that just as Christ was raised from the dead by the glory of the Father, even so we also should walk in newness of life."

Rom. 6:4

I think the enemy knows the power of baptism more than we do. If someone is saved out of a satanic cult, the cult leaders are not too concerned if they have become Christians. The real thing they want to know is if they been baptized! They know that once they are baptized, their ability to keep them bound or to win them back is over. It is interesting that the issue of baptism is what matters when someone converts to Christianity from Islam. Once they are baptized, they can justify an "honor killing". Likewise in Orthodox Judaism, once their son or daughter is baptized, they often do a funeral as if they had died. I believe there is a powerful deliverance that takes place in the spirit realm through water baptism.

John and I have watched born again believers get delivered from many strongholds and demonic oppression that keeps trying to drag them back to "Egypt", back to their worldly behaviors and addictions. It is surprising how many people who are saved by the blood of Jesus and desire to lead godly lives have never been taught the importance of being water baptized, and live tormented by the enemy who still has a legal right to them in those areas. In baptism, we submit to the waters to break off all the things we were in agreement with in the world. We come up out of the waters believing that we have identified with the death, burial and resurrection power of Jesus, and by faith, believe that those demonic strongholds are now disarmed and floating in the waters. At this point in the Seder it is important to stop and reflect upon your own baptism remembering the strongholds of the world that were cut off from your life on that day. If you have already been baptized but did not understand the spiritual dynamics that were taking place, then this is a good time to appropriate what actually took place when you were buried under the water. If you have not been baptized I hope after reading this you will understand how vital it is to your deliverance and freedom.

At a Jewish baptism, known as a mikvah, there is always a witness. His job is two-fold. First, he makes sure the person being baptized is fully immersed and second, he is a constant reminder to them that if Satan tries to pull them back into their old ways that he has no more legal right to them. The waters now separate him from those old habits and ways of the world. You cannot go to a grave of a "dead" person and bring him back. If that was all there was to the 3rd cup of redemption, we could rejoice and be glad, but there is even more to celebrate in this cup! In order to get the full impact of what I'm about to share I would like to briefly remind you of some of the customs that are part of an ancient Jewish wedding ceremony.

A father, or someone acting on behalf of the father (as in the story of Isaac and Rebekah), chooses a bride for his son. The son then goes to the bride-to-be's house, taking with him a skin of wine, a sum of money (called a "mohar" or bride price), and a gift for the bride. First the parents of the bride are asked for permission to marry, and if they agree the bride-to-be is brought out. A cup of wine is poured, called a betrothal cup. If the bride agrees, she drinks the cup of wine with the bridegroom. Then a "ketubah", a legal contract is signed, and the price for the bride is paid. He leaves a gift for the bride as a promise of his return and now they are legally married and would have to get a divorce to dissolve it.

The groom goes away, usually for a year, to build a bridal chamber to take her to. When his father has inspected it and it meets his specifications, a shofar is blown, and the bridegroom with four men carrying a palanquin, (a carriage carried on their shoulders to carry the bride back to the grooms house), begin the processional by announcing, "Behold the bridegroom cometh!" The bridegroom is known as a "thief in the night" because he usually arrives at the bride's house at midnight to "abduct the bride". He then carries her to his prepared bridal chamber and drinks another cup of wine with her called, "the cup of consummation". They then go in and consummate the marriage for seven days. Now with that in mind, let's turn to Luke.

> *"Then He said to them, "With fervent desire I have desired to eat this Passover with you before I suffer; for I say to you, I will no longer eat of it until it is fulfilled in the kingdom of God." Then He took the cup, and gave thanks, and said, "Take this and divide it among yourselves; for I say to you, I will not drink of the fruit of the vine until the kingdom of God comes."*
>
> *Luke 22:15-18*

> *"But I say to you, I will not drink of this fruit of the vine from now on until that day when I drink it new with you in My Father's kingdom."*
>
> *Matt. 26:29*

> *"Assuredly, I say to you, I will no longer drink of the fruit of the vine until that day when I drink it new in the kingdom of God."*
>
> *Mark 14:25*

Jesus said "with fervent desire" He wanted to celebrate this particular Passover with the ones He loved. It was an appointment He carried in His heart and was looking forward to for a long time. What was it about this Passover that was different? The answer is found in Luke 22:20. It states that Jesus took the cup after supper. The cup at a Passover Seder that is taken after the meal is the third cup. It is the cup of redemption. The disciples were familiar with this cup until Jesus did something very unusual. All of a sudden He took the traditional third cup and started talking marriage language! All the disciples present were Jewish men so they were very familiar with the customs of an ancient Jewish wedding. Jesus held the 3rd cup in His hand and turned it into a betrothal cup!

> *All of a sudden He took the traditional third cup and started talking marriage language!*

Remember, we just said that an ancient Jewish wedding had two parts. After the cup of betrothal, the bridegroom would be "like a man going away on a journey" until the bridal chamber, or "chuppah" was built and the bridegroom would return for the bride and then the second cup would conclude the second part of the wedding, called the consummation. I have read about these two marriage cups in Jewish literature that document the authenticity of this ancient tradition. The following quote is one example:

"One blessing over wine precedes the betrothal ceremony, another the nuptials ceremony. Because the two ceremonies retain their own integrity even though

united, two cups of wine should be used for the two blessings over wine… since in ancient times the betrothal took place in the bride's home and the nuptials in the groom's (at different times), the two separate cups recall that history."

www.chabad.org, wine

It was in this context that Jesus referred to when He was lifting the 3rd cup for them to take together after the meal, but the 4th cup, the cup of consummation, He would not drink until the day He came again to take His bride to the wedding chuppah! And where was He going?

Jesus said to them in *John 14:2,*

"In My Father's house are many mansions; if it were not so, I would have told you. I go to prepare a place for you. And if I go and prepare a place for you, I will come again and receive you to Myself; that where I am, there you may be also."

The magnitude of what He was doing must have blown the disciples' minds. They were busy thinking about what positions of leadership and power they would soon have now that the Messiah of Israel had finally come to set them free from their earthly oppressors, and He was initiating "a new covenant, written on their hearts"… a covenant of wedding betrothal… drinking a cup of wine to make it legal and

> *He was initiating "a new covenant, written on their hearts"… a covenant of wedding betrothal*

172

Finding the Afikoman

eating the broken matzah, the afikoman (meaning the satisfaction)... the last thing eaten at a Passover Seder!

I want to insert the explanation of this verse where I quoted it in chapter 3:

> *"And Jesus said to them, "Can the friends of the bridegroom fast while the bridegroom is with them?' As long as they have the bridegroom with them they cannot fast. But the days will come when the bridegroom will be taken away from them, and then they will fast in those days."*
>
> *Mark 2:19-20*

Jesus said, "Do this in remembrance of Me". What are we to remember every time we do communion? That we are legally betrothed and right now we have a Bridegroom in heaven that is interceding for His bride and preparing a place to take us when He returns! He paid the bride price (mohar) with His own blood and then at the next Spring feast of Shavuot (Pentecost), He left a gift for His bride: the indwelling Holy Spirit! *Hebrews 12:2 says, "...for the joy that was set before Him He endured the cross...".* What was that joy??? It was us! He saw beyond the cross, the payment to "buy us back", and saw that day when He would finally have the reward of six thousand years of suffering, since the enemy stole His bride in the garden. This is not a fairy tale. This is real and we get to be part of it. So we can partake of this cup together,

173

remembering what He remembers: *"...The love of your betrothal, When you went after Me in the wilderness..." (Jer. 2:2).* Every Passover, and every time we take communion we can lift our cup and say "yes" to Him again!

Don't you feel excited? Doesn't the beauty of this pattern make you look forward to gathering your family and friends every year and keep this appointment with the Lord? Wouldn't it be amazing to have a specific time each year on His calendar to celebrate your salvation and deliverance with others and rejoice in what the Lord has done and continues to do in your lives? Not in the spirit of bondage or legalism that imposes a "heavy yoke" that comes with a religious spirit, but in expectation and freedom knowing that He is a living God and no two Passovers will be the same.

• The fourth cup or the forth, "I will" is •

"I will take you as My people, and I will be your God..."
Ex.6:7

The last cup at Passover is called "the cup of consummation" and is taken from the last "I will" in Exodus 6:7. I am not going to share on the fourth cup in this chapter. The first 3 cups were the steps of our salvation, deliverance and redemption out of "Egypt". They are the necessary experiences that He takes us through to make us a new creation. The fourth cup is our destination, and is so incredibly full of revelation and meaning that I wrote a whole chapter on it. The next stop for the children of Israel was on a mountain to enter into a marriage covenant with God. The fourth cup is part of the last spring feast call Shavuot. I am sure by now it won't surprise you to know that Shavuot is also about a wedding! From slaves, to sons, to a kingdom of priests, to a bride... that sums up in a nutshell the pattern of the four cups of redemption. Amazing.

Someone recently asked the question, "Do we have to keep the Jewish festivals as Gentile believers? That seems so legalistic." With the Holy Spirit grieving within me, knowing the gift God has left us to meet with Him at these appointed times that not only reveal the secrets of His two visits to earth, but unlock the deep well of His love for us and the glorious plan of redemption that He looks forward to in the future; I answered, "We don't have to, but we will be honored, privileged and blessed in this lifetime if we get to."

"The stars do not move You,
the waves can't undo you,
the mountains in their splendor
can not steal your heart.
This God Who is holy, perfect in beauty,
awesome in glory,
is ravished by my heart.
Somehow my weak glance has overwhelmed You,
somehow my weak love,
has stolen away Your heart."

Sarah Edwards

~ Chapter 6 ~

Shavuot

"…The king has brought me into his chambers…"
Song of Songs 1:4

As I sit down to write this chapter on Shavuot, I am smiling as I whisper to the Lord saying, "We have had a lot of memories together over the years with this one!" I feel He is smiling in agreement. I pressed into the revelation and meaning of this feast for many years with great cost emotionally, spiritually and even financially, but for 35 years it still remained just some good information void of His heart. I hated this holiday. I had asked and asked and obediently kept it but it was anti-climactic after the heart encounters that we experienced during Passover. Our friends' hearts would come alive as they encountered Jesus in the Passover and would ask with excitement if we could do the next feast together; I would think, "Shavuot… ugh, not that one" and would hope they would forget. Finally in 2011 and then again in 2012, He suddenly revealed to me a few glimpses into His emotions that are attached to this sacred "appointed time". I will attempt to share with you my unfolding history in discovery of this feast. It now

177

holds a tender place in my heart, filling me with awe and a very reverent fear of the Lord.

In the beginning of my journey, my Greek thinking used to compartmentalize the feasts as if one would end and then the next one would begin. If we do that and approach the feasts like subjects in school that are not integrated, we risk losing the cohesive flow of God's divine love story from Genesis through Revelation. We have to see the intensity and passion... the heart of righteous justice and holy indignation that has been set in motion... when He paid the price in full, for the Bride that is rightfully His. It is a terrifying force for anything or anyone who gets in His way. If our Christian faith is without this reality, without this understanding of this epic love story, the Bible becomes boring and we end up in dead religion. It was the discovery of the unfolding love story hidden in the festivals that kept my heart alive and wanting more of Him.

The whole purpose for me sharing my story with others is not to teach information. I didn't pursue knowledge; I pursued intimacy and knowledge of Him. Most of what I am sharing I learned by the Holy Spirit leading me one step at a time, and is taken from my private journals that I never thought I would ever be sharing. It took much prompting from Him to even be willing to share the secrets of His heart to mine. But it is His story, His glory, and if any of this leads you into intimacy resulting in loving Him more, then it will be worth it all.

> *I didn't pursue knowledge; I pursued intimacy and knowledge of Him*

Review of the Four Cups of Redemption

The Passover initiated His deliverance and redemption of a people He had chosen to be His special treasure. God didn't annihilate a nation just to get a people out of slavery to an evil world system and leader. Likewise, Jesus did not come to earth as a Man and suffer an agonizing death just to save us out of Hell. Both the drama of Exodus and the events of the first coming of Jesus 1500 years later, had a specific purpose that was established at the foundation of the world: God lost an intimate partner to the enemy, Satan, in the Garden of Eden. In the book of Genesis, He set a plan in motion to get her back. We best not diminish this to the level of a nice fairy tale. Having said all that, let's remember where He left our hearts after the Passover Seder. Focusing on the four cups of redemption, we clearly saw how the pattern walked out by the children of Israel in the book of Exodus were the same steps our Lord Jesus takes each of us through to lead us into a relationship with Himself. As we took the first cup of Exodus 6:6-7, we remembered how He sovereignly made us see our bondage in the world, and seeing it we hated it and cried out to be free. We remembered the God who not only produces the cry to make us quit tolerating our bondage, past and present, but we see that He also answers that cry and comes to our rescue.

With cup number two we experienced that the way out of Egypt was by the blood of the lamb on the doorposts in Exodus, and the precious blood of Jesus 1500 years later. We also saw that, in addition to salvation and deliverance, the blood of the lamb healed their bodies so there were none sick or lame among them, *Ps. 105:37,* *"He also brought them out with silver and gold, and there was none feeble among His tribes."* Discovering this verse we realized that the second cup of deliverance also had the power to heal our bodies.

After the meal we drank cup number three, the amazing cup of redemption. This is the cup where we saw the children of Israel pass through the waters of the Red Sea and they transferred from one kingdom to another… from one taskmaster's ownership to be the possession of their loving Redeemer. In this cup we saw the power of water baptism that disarms principalities and powers that held us in bondage and want to keep pursuing us after we are saved. It is in the watery grave of the Red Sea that Pharaoh and his army are legally dealt with and likewise, our water baptism is the place where our old man with all his worldly ways is reckoned dead.

If the third cup had nothing else to experience, it would have been enough, but after that, we learned what Jesus did at the Passover Seder with His disciples the night before He died! We saw in the word how He suddenly changed the traditional third Passover cup into a betrothal cup and started using language that a Jewish Bridegroom would use! If you do not remember the details, please read the appendix at the back of the book about this amazing third cup of redemption and let your heart be romanced again at the profound moment when Jesus revealed the reason for the "joy set before Him" that enabled Him to pay the bride price with His own blood! The revelation of this will make us feel born again, again!

The Fourth Cup

That takes us up to the fourth cup. Jesus did not partake of the fourth cup with His disciples. He turned the third cup into a betrothal cup and, like a typical Jewish bridegroom would do. He then said that He was going to prepare a place to take them and would not partake again of a cup of wine until His Father's kingdom when He comes for them: ***"But I say to you, I will not drink of this fruit of the vine from now on until that day when I drink it new with you in My Father's kingdom." (Matt. 26:29).***

The fourth cup at the Passover Seder is called the cup of consummation and is the last "I will" from ***Exodus 6:6-7: "…I will take you as My people…".*** Remember in the ancient Jewish wedding ceremony that we talked about in the first session, after the betrothal cup was drunk by the bride who agreed to this legally binding contract, the bridegroom would go build a wedding chamber or chuppah in His father's house to bring his bride to when it was completed. On that day in the future that only the father knew, he would take her to the wedding chuppah and drink the last cup of wine together called the cup of consummation. Then they would consummate the wedding for seven days.

At the end of our Passover Seders that John and I would host, I was always left feeling that the last cup got neglected. It is drunk right after the third cup which is so rich with meaning and heart encounter that it never seemed right to quench the glow of that moment by moving on to the last cup. Consequently, I would mention the fourth cup, say it is the cup of consummation and then mumble a few shallow sentences that usually go unnoticed after a long, full evening of food, wine and new revelation. The fourth cup was to remain a hidden piece to the puzzle for a while but now I will show you how I followed the road to where the buried treasure of Jesus, the Afikoman (the satisfaction), was finally found regarding the fourth cup, so appropriately named, "the cup of consummation". By the end of this chapter I will tell you more about what I have uncovered about this cup of redemption, but to get there, I have to take you on my trail discovering Shavuot.

My Journey Discovering Shavuot

I am a visual learner. The Holy Spirit speaks to me in pictures. The first "picture" of Shavuot that I saw was in my mother-in-law's synagogue when I was first seeking Him for the meaning of this festival. I walked in the door to the sanctuary and was struck with the beauty of it. Flowers and greenery were everywhere. The sun was streaming in the windows with rays of light shining on the front podium and highlighting two gigantic loaves of braided challah bread. It was gorgeous and I remember thinking that surely it was set up for a wedding! It so made an impression on my emotions that now, more than three decades later, I remember it vividly.

I had read in Jewish books from the library that Shavuot was one of the three annual pilgrim feasts in ancient Israel. Three times a year, on Passover, Shavuot, and Sukkot (the Feast of Tabernacles), the children of Israel were required to come from all the surrounding nations to celebrate together in Jerusalem. I read that on Shavuot, because it fell in May/June on our Gregorian calendar, the flowers were in bloom, the hillsides around Jerusalem were green with new spring growth and it was the wheat harvest. Right before this holiday began, the farmers would go into their fields, bundle the first new stalks of wheat and tie them with red ribbon to mark them for the first fruits of the wheat harvest. A few days later at the start of Shavuot, they were cut and taken to the temple in Jerusalem to be offered, or waved, before the Lord. I learned that this feast commemorated the day that the children of Israel were first given the Torah on Mt. Sinai and entered into a covenant with God. Because of this, devout Jews would stay up all night reading the scriptures together, focusing on the book of Ruth because her story unfolded between the barley and the wheat harvest. The large loaves of bread in the synagogue were the picture of the fullness of the wheat harvest at Shavuot.

So these were the pictures I held in my heart: the synagogue decked out for a wedding, and the beautiful scene I pictured from ancient Israel. I pictured caravans of Jews streaming in to Jerusalem, their wagons full of grain and fruit offerings to the Lord… coming into Jerusalem and seeing the hillsides dotted with red ribbons tied around the sheaves of wheat… spring in the air… hope renewed… rejoicing with each other… singing and dancing, celebrating the God of Israel and the blessings He had bestowed upon them! Wow, what an amazing prophetic picture of the Kingdom of God! It was so profound to me that I wanted to enter into it. I wanted to create that picture, and then surely He would show up and encounter my heart with revelation of Himself in the midst of it! What happened next will either be seen as a totally delusional ego trip, or what might have been just an immature yet sincere, child-like heart that was zealous to find Him. Only God knows.

Together with our good friends, Bob and Donna, and my poor husband that went along with all my wild and irrational schemes, we attempted to recreate the picture of Shavuot in ancient Israel that I carried in my mind's eye. We rented a large banquet room for the date of Shavuot in the Chilson Community Center in downtown Loveland, Colorado where we lived. We then spent the next six weeks preparing and building and brainstorming to set up the old city of Jerusalem with the Temple in the middle of the room!

We made 8 ft. high walls of plywood and cut out arches to look like the Eastern gate. We sponge painted what were supposed to be Jerusalem stones on brown postal paper that we hung on the plywood. We gathered flowers, palm trees, vines and greenery. We tied wheat stalks with red ribbons for the centerpieces placed next to overflowing fruit baskets. We hung purple balloons with green strings on poles to look like grapes from the Promised Land with a path through the room that led to our "temple" so that after the meal each of our 100 guests could take their family inside and take communion together. At the end of the evening we pictured ourselves gathered together in the middle of the room, tied with red ribbon, offering ourselves up as sheaves of wheat before the Father and asking Him to pour out His Spirit like He did when He fulfilled this festival of Shavuot (Pentecost in Greek) in the second chapter of Acts. It was, no doubt, going to be a life-changing evening!

Now thirty years later, remembering this event makes me feel exhausted! It took enormous time, energy and money to pull this off but all I can say is, at the time, the preparation was glorious. I felt the presence of His Spirit so strong each step of the way and we felt His extravagance to give it our all. Our friend and spiritual father, Tim Ruthven was excited to learn the Jewish feasts with us so he was coming to share that evening and said that his whole time of preparation, like ours, was filled with a holy expectation of His presence.

At this same time, we rented an office space in an old downtown shop a few blocks away and had been praying a year with Bob and Donna for God to pour out His Spirit in our city. Before you are impressed with our spiritual zeal, it was honestly one of the most oppressive things we have done. Our prayers were un-anointed, our hearts were dull, and we mostly slept and killed flies on the window sills. Only God knows if our dead prayers took flight and accomplished anything for His kingdom in Loveland, Colorado. We did, however, feel an increased expectancy as we prayed for 6 weeks leading up to our Shavuot party. We felt it, Tim felt it; God was going to pour out His spirit in our rented room that we had prepared!

I can still remember the feeling that night when everything was ready. The room was beautiful. The tables were set with white tablecloths and the candles on each table gave an inviting ambiance with the fruit baskets and bright red ribbon tied around the tall wheat sheaves. There, in the middle of the room was our crowning glory... the temple with candles dimly glowing on the table inside, with palm trees and flowers, and our huge "grapes" adorning the outside. The atmosphere felt electric with His presence. Surely the Lord was in this place! Then something terrible happened and the atmosphere totally changed; the guests started to arrive. It was like someone took a pin and popped a balloon. One minute I felt like Cinderella at the ball being romanced by a handsome prince decked out in a beautiful dress, and in a moment, I was in rags running home on foot after my carriage had turned into a pumpkin.

When people came through the door, our temple looked like a shabby lean-to, the grapes were rapidly deflating balloons, the whole room looked tacky and over the top ridiculous. I felt like Bozo the clown with a big, red nose and I wanted desperately to run out of the room. It was horrible. John mumbled a few things and then Tim shared something that made no sense and later he said he felt like the anointing and expectation he was carrying for weeks leaked out the bottom of his shoes! We somehow got through the evening and I went home that night tired, disappointed, humiliated and mad at God for abandoning us. I lay in bed that night, tears streaming down my cheeks and told Him, "I am never going to do that again! Where did you go? What was that all about???" I felt Him say, "I loved it." I asked, "You loved it?? Why?" He said, "I loved looking down from heaven and seeing a picture of Me; a testimony of Me in the midst of a city. It gave Me pleasure. Thank you." Have you ever felt like even though your mind feels dumb, your spirit somehow gets it? That was one of those moments and all I could say was, "You are welcome," but at the same time never wanting to go near this festival again!

After that evening I focused on the other feasts and had to put Shavuot on the shelf for a while. I knew there was so much more than what I had seen so far, but I had to leave it alone until He said it was time to take it down again. When it came around each year we would bake the challah and have the traditional dairy food meals, and a few years attempted to stay up all night to read the word but barely got through the book of Ruth before we called it a night.

I felt a little bit of a spark again when I was given a written account from the Talmud, taken from Jewish historians about what they say happened in Exodus 19 when God brought the children of Israel to Mt. Sinai. (This is the same one I mentioned above in **Appendix H**) In short, they described the dramatic event with wind and the thundering of God's voice in seventy known languages and tongues of fire on the mountain! It was God's invitation to the nations to make a covenant with Him but only the nation of Israel said yes. It is so strikingly similar to the experience the disciples had in Acts chapter two, that it is easy to see that on this same holiday of Shavuot that was initiated in Exodus 19, the Lord came and fulfilled it perfectly 1500 years later. The fact that Jewish writings, that do not want to line up with the New Testament, coincide with what is written by Paul and other New Testament writers is astounding to me and makes me trust in their validity.

In 1999 I was reading a book called, <u>The Jewish Way</u> by Rabbi Irving Greenberg. I love this book and highly recommend it to anyone wanting to see the heart of the festivals rather than mere information. It is one of the Jewish books that I believe the Holy Spirit highlighted to me when I needed to understand the Jewish mindset and philosophy of life. At this time, I was finding wedding language in many of the festivals and it was getting my attention. I was reading Rabbi Greenberg's chapter on Shavuot, and came to an interesting section (pp. 82-84). He is talking about modern customs surrounding this holiday and mentioned that some Jews stay awake all night preparing for the wedding to God on Mt. Sinai, and saw it **"as time to prepare the bride's trousseau for the wedding (with God) in the morning." (Rabbi Irving**

Greenberg, The Jewish Way, p. 82). They would then have a mock wedding ceremony the next day, renewing their covenantal wedding vows between themselves and the Lord. When I read that I asked the Holy Spirit if that was what was really happening on Mt. Sinai in Exodus 19. Was it more than the giving of the law? If it was yet another picture of a wedding like I had been seeing in some of the other feasts, then I was intrigued, to say the least!

Progression of Our Identity Change in Exodus

I read Exodus 19 over a few times looking for clues. Then I saw it! All at once it became clear what was happening on that mountain!

Cup #1

- He called slaves to hate their bondage

- *"And the LORD said: "I have surely seen the oppression of my people who are in Egypt, and I have heard their cry because of their taskmasters, for I know their sorrows." Ex. 3:7*

- *"...I am the LORD, I will bring you out from under the burdens (tolerance) of the Egyptians." Ex. 6:6*

Cup #2

- He called His son (1st Israel, then Jesus) out of Egypt.

- *"When Israel was a child, I loved him, And out of Egypt I called My son." Hosea 11:1*

- *"and was there until the death of Herod, that it might be fulfilled which was spoken by the Lord through the prophet, saying, "Out of Egypt I called My Son." Matt. 2:15*

Cup #3

- He redeemed them back from the enemy and brought them to the wilderness as priests.

- *"You have seen what I did to the Egyptians, and how I bore you on eagles' wings and brought you to Myself. Now therefore, if you will indeed obey My voice and keep My covenant, then you shall be a special treasure to Me above all people; for all the earth is Mine. And you shall be to Me a kingdom of priests and a holy nation..." Ex. 19:4-6*

Cup #4

- He brought them to a mountain to be His betrothed bride.

- *"Go and cry in the hearing of Jerusalem, saying, 'Thus says the LORD: "I remember you, The kindness of your youth, The love of your betrothal, When you went after Me in the wilderness, In a land not sown." Jer. 2:2*

Marriage on the Mountain

The fourth step of our redemption from **Exodus 6:6-7** is, *"...I will take you as My people, and I will be your God."* God did not save the children of Israel out of Egypt just to free them from bondage. He had more than deliverance in mind even more than redeeming, or buying us back, from the enemy. That was part of what was accomplished, first in Egypt and then, 1500 years later, when Jesus came to die for us. But if that is all we see, then we have a very self-centered view of our salvation story. It is not mainly about what we benefit from what He accomplished for us; but instead what He gets. He was the One that lost His partner in the garden. He is the One Who is desiring His bride back. He was the One Who paid the price for her unfaithfulness and suffered the injustice of the innocent dying for the guilty. He is the One Who deserves the full reward of not only the suffering of the cruel death of being nailed to a cross, but the grief and anguish of 6,000 years of being a scorned bridegroom.

In Exodus 19 the children of Israel appeared before God at Mt. Sinai and were consecrated three days. On the third day, God appeared in a frightening display of power that we read about in the Jewish historical account of that very first Shavuot; wind, lightning, tongues of fire, thundering, and a thick cloud of His presence that came down. It would have been terrifying if you did not know Him or, if you did not know His intention for bringing them there. He had Moses tell them a tender word about carrying them on eagles' wings out of Egypt to be a holy nation of priests, a special treasure to Him out of all the nations of the world. There was a loud shofar blast to summon this bride to the mountain. It was referred to in Exodus 19:

> *"Then it came to pass on the third day, in the morning, that there were thunderings and lightnings, and a thick cloud on the mountain; and the sound of the trumpet was very loud, so that all the people who were in the camp trembled. And Moses brought the people out of the camp to meet with God, and they stood at the foot of the mountain. Now Mount Sinai was completely in smoke, because the LORD descended upon it in fire. Its smoke ascended like the smoke of a furnace, and the whole mountain quaked greatly. And when the blast of the trumpet sounded long and became louder and louder, Moses spoke, and God answered him by voice."*
>
> *Ex.19:16-19*

Three Important Shofar Blasts

Judaism has three main shofar blasts. The one blown at Shavuot in this verse is called the "first trump". The one blown at the first fall feast of Yom Teruah (Rosh Hashana) is called the "last trump". The one blown at Yom Kippur is called the "great trump". They are all recorded in scripture and are still blown to this day. We will talk more about those when we come to the fall feasts. Just to get your curiosity going, I will tell you that they are all part of a wedding ceremony! Hopefully you will want to read the second book, ***Watching and Waiting: Discovering Jesus in the Fall Feasts***.

Marriage Covenant at Sinai

On Mt. Sinai God was basically inviting a people into a marriage covenant. It was if God was saying, "I have taken you, Israel, to be my special people, My bride. If you, in turn, take Me to be your God, say, 'I do'". The people responded with their "yes" in the following verse:

> *"Then all the people answered together and said, "All that the LORD has spoken we will do." So Moses brought back the words of the people to the LORD."*
>
> *Ex. 19:8*

We read in Deuteronomy 28 the blessings and the curses. Basically God was saying to them: "I am taking you this day to be My people. If you agree to take Me to be your God, here is how I will take care of you as your Bridegroom. If you are a faithful bride and love Me by keeping this marriage covenant, then all the blessings listed in Deuteronomy 28 are yours. But, if you are unfaithful to Me, all the curses listed will come upon you. If you leave Me for other gods, I will make you so miserable that even if you try to desperately sell yourselves as slaves in Egypt, you will be so grotesque that even they will not take you. Then, you will have to come back to Me and when you do, I will restore and bless all that you have lost and will love you." This was a binding contract and God was warning them that He takes their agreement very seriously. He was warning them not to say "I do" unless they intended to be faithful to Him.

The people agreed to what I believe, was the first part of a wedding contract that was legally binding and that was the betrothal. The betrothal in an ancient Jewish wedding had a written contract called a ketubah. The Lord left the contract behind, which is called the Ten Commandments. But here is the interesting part. The second part of the wedding ceremony is in the bridal chamber, or chuppah where it is consummated.

The Mystery of the Fourth Cup Revealed

The people were afraid to go up, Moses went up in the cloud and God came down. Moses ate with Him on a sea of glass on the mountain. I will not

Moses went up in the cloud and God came down

comment on this now, but just hold on to that picture because it is very significant for you to see this as part of your future story as well. Just as a reminder though, I will leave you with this. Right now, in the heavenly Jerusalem, Jesus is constructing a bridal chamber to take you to one day. He took the third cup of betrothal and said in *John 14:2-3,*

> *"In My Father's house are many mansions; if it were not so, I would have told you. I go to prepare a place for you.*

And if I go and prepare a place for you, I will come again and receive you to Myself; that where I am, there you may be also."

He also said He would not take the fourth cup with them until His Father's kingdom, (Matt. 26:29). I believe He was alluding to the consummation in the chuppah that He was taking us to one day where that last cup of wine would be shared between the bride and groom.

This explains why the fourth cup at a Passover Seder has always seemed inappropriate to take at that time. I felt bad rushing through it at the end, but felt that to say much about it would quench what the Spirit was doing with the third cup. Now I was to understand why Jesus did not drink it either. It is reserved for another time in a special place that He is preparing for us, even now! Even as I am writing this, I am saying to myself, "Do you understand what you just wrote???"

All these years of doing Passover Seders and feeling guilty that I had not done the fourth cup justice, is suddenly making sense to me. The four cups of redemption are labeled according to the four "I wills" found in the verses from Exodus 6:6-7. The first three cups are the steps to save and deliver the Israelites from Egypt (and us from this world system under Satan) but the forth cup stands alone. It is not part of the actions God initiates to save and deliver us; rather it is the goal of our salvation. It is the reason for the divine rescue mission in the first place. God wants a partner and He has set His affections on us. He is taking us out, cleaning us up, and setting us aside as holy and spotless, "a bride adorned for her Husband".

Remember, there are two cups taken at two different times in a Jewish wedding. First is the cup of betrothal, and then, the cup of consummation which the bride and groom drink together in the bridal chamber or chuppah where they stay together and physically become one flesh. As we said in the last chapter, Jesus was doing a traditional Passover Seder with His disciples before His death, until the third cup after the meal, referred to in Luke 22:20. Remember, He turned that cup into a betrothal cup, which it was always meant to be at His fulfillment, and said He was going to prepare a place to take them to Himself and He would not drink another cup until He brought us to heaven one day.

In other words, Jesus was saying, "that last cup of consummation that you drink every year at the end of the Seder meal, this time I am not drinking it with you because it has been in this ceremony to be rehearsed for the last 1500 years until I came and fulfilled it." It's interesting to note that the Hebrew word for fulfill means to properly walk it out, or properly interpret it. An example of this is in **Matt 5:17, "Do not think that I came to destroy the Law or the Prophets. I did not come to destroy but to fulfill."** It was as if Jesus was saying,

> *"This ceremony has been rehearsed all these years so that when I actually came to earth I could keep this appointment. Now you are betrothed to me after drinking the third cup and all those who come after you who believe in Me will be betrothed also. But from now on, do not drink the last cup. It was named the cup of consummation because it really is! Did you ever wonder why it was named this? Just think of what Exodus 6:7 is saying; I will bring you to Myself... I am going away now to build a bridal chamber but when I come again, I will bring you to Myself... to this*

place in heaven that I am leaving to build... and we will then drink this cup of consummation like they do at every Jewish wedding."

Wow! Now I understood why every Passover Seder we had done for the past 38 years always felt finished after we celebrated the third cup of redemption. Jesus did not drink the fourth cup with His disciples because He was saving it for that special day, sometime in the future, when He comes again, to take His bride (that He paid for with His blood), and complete part two of the marriage covenant. It was a relief to know that we were not neglecting this cup every year, but rather, He was actually saying, "It is not yet time."

Moses walked the children of Israel to the mountain to be legally betrothed on the first Shavuot recorded in the Bible. Then Moses walked up the mountain, disappeared with the Lord in a cloud and experienced the consummation. The cloud came down and Moses met Him in the cloud! (Ex.19:20, Ex. 24:15-18) Hold onto that picture because Revelation 1:7 says Jesus is coming in clouds! Moses was the forerunner, the first to keep the pattern of the spring feasts in the book of Exodus. Then Jesus, "a Prophet like Moses," came, walked through, fulfilled, and will continue to fulfill, the exact same pattern. Moses then walked through the pattern of the fall feasts from Exodus 19- 34, which I will share with you when we get to the fall festivals. Sometime in the future, Jesus will follow and do likewise. It is all too amazing for words to describe.

Revelation of God's Heart, 2012

In the spring of 2012, I had a revelation of Him in Shavuot that I believe is a key to understanding His heart that is expressed through the writing of the prophets. I was asked to teach a small class on the festivals and we had just finished experiencing the beautiful story of redemption and deliverance that is in the Passover Seder. They could not wait to hear my teaching on Shavuot and I was not feeling much life on it. I could share the wedding picture that Rabbi Greenberg had helped me to see in Exodus 19, and that was good, but I ached to know more. We can strive to understand something in the word but try as we might, head knowledge just isn't the same as those pearls of revelation understanding that just suddenly come and you know that you are getting something you could never have seen on your own. That is what happened twenty minutes before I walked into class to teach on Shavuot.

I was sitting in my car and said to the Lord, "I know there is something more to this feast, I have felt that for years but I don't get it. Where is your heart in it?" Almost instantly I felt Him answer, and what He said still makes me cry every time I share it. He said, "It is where I made My heart vulnerable." I sat there stunned. What? How can God ever be vulnerable to man? Impossible. Unthinkable. But then the revelation began to unfold. I hope you stop and pause and take in what I am about to say because this is not theology or information; this is about God's feelings and the magnitude of it is absolutely heartbreaking.

> "It is where I made My heart vulnerable."

From what I can see in scripture, up until this moment on Mt. Sinai God had not revealed Himself as a

197

Bridegroom. It is a rich study to look at how God reveals His character through His different names at strategic times in the Old Testament. I would highly recommend reading The Names of God by Andrew Jukes. It is another tool that the Lord used to help me get to know Him more intimately. We see that He is Elohim, the mighty creator God in Genesis, Who is in covenant with all that He created. Then, later in Genesis, He appears to Abraham in a tender way and calls him His friend and reveals Himself as El Elyon, the "Lord Most High", ruler over heaven and earth. We see the revelation of Jehovah (YHWH), working mighty signs and wonders, delivering the children of Israel from Egypt with a mighty outstretched arm and yet demanding righteousness and holiness, and warns Israel not to worship other gods,

> *"...For I, the LORD (Jehovah) your God, am a jealous God, visiting the iniquity of the fathers upon the children to the third and fourth generations of those who hate Me, but showing mercy to thousands, to those who love Me and keep My commandments."*
> *Ex. 20:5-6, parenthesis added*

As El Shaddai, He reveals His provision and protection in the wilderness after delivering His people out of Egypt. Andrew Jukes says,

> **"This is El Shaddai, the 'Pourer-forth,' Who pours Himself out for His creatures; Who gives them His life-blood; Who**

'sheds forth His spirit,' and says, 'come unto Me and drink; Open your mouth wide and I will fill it.'"
Andrew Jukes, <u>Names of God</u>, p.69

He is their cloud by day and their fire by night. He feeds them manna to eat and brings forth water from a rock, while protecting them from all their enemies.

Then He takes them to a mountain, *("I will take you as My people..." (Ex. 6:7)*), and something astonishing happens. He legally betroths His people to Himself; and just like the requirement in an ancient wedding ceremony, once the bride agrees, the contract (called a ketubah) is written down by the groom (the 10 commandments), and from that day on the covenant of marriage is legal. Looking through this lens you can now read Deuteronomy 28, the blessings and curses, and understand God's promise of blessing to a faithful bride and His warning of judgment to an unfaithful one.

Once He becomes a Bridegroom, everything changes. Any man who is married can understand this vulnerability that the bride you marry holds your heart in their hand and if they leave to go after another you could be devastated. This is what Israel did to the Lord, and the anguish of God's broken heart over His unfaithful wife is heard throughout the writing of the prophets. Let's read some of these and let your heart feel God's emotions in light of this perspective.

"Go and cry in the hearing of Jerusalem, saying, 'Thus says the Lord: "I remember you, The kindness of your youth, The love of your betrothal, When you went after me

199

in the wilderness, In a land not sown...Thus says the LORD: "What injustice have your fathers found in Me, That they have gone far from Me, Have followed idols, And have become idolaters? Neither did they say, 'Where is the LORD, Who brought us up out of the land of Egypt, Who led us through the wilderness, Through a land of deserts and pits, Through a land of drought and the shadow of death, Through a land that no one crossed And where no one dwelt?'"

Jer. 2:2, 5-6

"Surely, as a wife treacherously departs from her husband, So have you dealt treacherously with Me, O house of Israel," *says the LORD."*

Jer. 3:20

"Then those of you who escape will remember Me among the nations where they are carried captive, because I was crushed by their adulterous heart which has departed from me, and by their eyes which play the harlot after their idols; they will loathe themselves for the evils which they committed in their abominations."

Ez. 6:9

"Again the word of the Lord came to me, saying, "Son of man, cause Jerusalem to know her abominations, and say, 'Thus

says the Lord God to Jerusalem: "Your birth and your nativity are from the land of Canaan; your father was an Amorite and your mother a Hittite. As for your nativity, on the day you were born your navel cord was not cut, nor were you washed in water to cleanse you; you were not rubbed with salt nor wrapped in swaddling clothes. No eye pitied you, to do any of these things for you, to have compassion on you; but you were thrown out into the open field, when you yourself were loathed on the day you were born. "And when I passed by you and saw you struggling in your own blood, I said to you in your blood, 'Live!' Yes, I said to you in your blood, 'Live!' I made you thrive like a plant in the field; and you grew, matured, and became very beautiful. Your breasts were formed, your hair grew, but you were naked and bare. "When I passed by you again and looked upon you, indeed your time was the time of love; so I spread My wing over you and covered your nakedness. Yes, I swore an oath to you and entered into a covenant with you, and you became Mine," says the Lord God. "Then I washed you in water; yes, I thoroughly washed off your blood, and I anointed you with oil. I clothed you in embroidered cloth and gave you sandals of badger skin; I clothed you with fine linen and covered you with silk. I adorned you with ornaments, put

201

bracelets on your wrists, and a chain on your neck. And I put a jewel in your nose, earrings in your ears, and a beautiful crown on your head. Thus you were adorned with gold and silver, and your clothing was of fine linen, silk, and embroidered cloth. You ate pastry of fine flour, honey, and oil. You were exceedingly beautiful, and succeeded to royalty. Your fame went out among the nations because of your beauty, for it was perfect through My splendor which I had bestowed on you," says the Lord God...You have also taken your beautiful jewelry from My gold and My silver, which I had given you, and made for yourself male images and played the harlot with them."

Ez. 16:1-14, 17

"You are an adulterous wife, who takes strangers instead of her husband...And I will judge you as women who break wedlock or shed blood are judged; I will bring blood upon you in fury and jealousy."

Ez. 16:32, 38

"For the Lord your God is a consuming fire, a jealous God."

Deut. 4:24

"Behold, the days are coming, says the Lord, when I will make a new covenant with the house of Israel and with the house of Judah—not according to the covenant that I made with their fathers in the day that I took them by the hand to lead them out of the land of Egypt, My covenant which they broke, though I was a husband to them, says the Lord. But this is the covenant that I will make with the house of Israel after those days, says the Lord: I will put My law in their minds, and write it on their hearts; and I will be their God, and they shall be My people. No more shall every man teach his neighbor, and every man his brother, saying, 'Know the Lord,' for they all shall know Me, from the least of them to the greatest of them, says the Lord. For I will forgive their iniquity, and their sin I will remember no more."

Jer. 31:31-34

"For your Maker is your husband, The Lord of hosts is His name; And your Redeemer is the Holy One of Israel; He is called the God of the whole earth. For the Lord has called you Like a woman forsaken and grieved in spirit, Like a youthful wife when you were refused," Says your God. *"For a mere moment I have forsaken you, But with great mercies I will gather you. With a little wrath I hid*

203

My face from you for a moment; But with everlasting kindness I will have mercy on you," Says the Lord, your Redeemer."

Is. 54:5-8

"And it shall be, in that day," Says the Lord, "That you will call Me 'My Husband,' And no longer call Me 'My Master,'... "I will betroth you to Me forever; Yes, I will betroth you to Me In righteousness and justice, In lovingkindness and mercy; I will betroth you to Me in faithfulness, And you shall know the Lord."

Hosea 2:16, 19-20

Don't think that God takes a marriage contract lightly! I will never forget one of my favorite Bible teachers talking about the Day of the Lord at the end of this age when Jesus comes to earth as a Bridegroom, King and Judge to remove anything and anyone who has stolen the love of His bride. In a booming, passionate voice he said, "Trust me when I say, there is no fury like that of a scorned lover!" God will do whatever it takes to win them back!

Do we think it is any different for us? We are betrothed to the Creator of the universe, the King of Kings. Every time we take communion we should remember that third cup that Jesus took with His disciples the night before He died. We need to encourage and strengthen our hearts with this bridal reality that we are a betrothed people! Jesus paid the bride price for us with His blood and left the bridal gift of His Spirit dwelling within us! He is serious about this covenant that cost Him everything... He is not going to lose His bride! He is building a bridal chamber and when the Father says it is ready, He is coming to get us! Because of this, when we take communion, let's rejoice as we remember this exhilarating truth. More than lowly sinners hoping to be worthy to take the cup; we are a redeemed bride being made spotless and proclaiming the Day coming when the shofar blast will sound and the proclamation is heard, "Behold, the Bridegroom cometh!"

The Counting of the Omer

When you follow the journey of the children of Israel from Exodus 12 to Exodus 19, you can see the pattern of the spring feasts that they walked out perfectly. Then they were written down by Moses in Leviticus 23 after God revealed the pattern to him on Mt. Sinai. They were to be walked out, rehearsed, and proclaimed so when the Messiah came to perfectly fulfill them we would not miss the time of his visitation. We have already established that the children of Israel came through the Red Sea and were raised onto dry ground the morning of the "moed" in Leviticus 23:9-14, called the first fruits of the barley harvest. Leviticus 23:15-16, 50 days later, is the Feast of Weeks or Shavuot (meaning weeks).

> *They were to be walked out, rehearsed, and proclaimed*

"And you shall count for yourselves from the day after the Sabbath, from the day that you brought the sheaf of the wave offering: seven Sabbaths shall be

*completed. Count fifty days to the day
after the seventh Sabbath; then you shall
offer a new grain offering to the LORD."*
Lev. 23:15-16

The time between these two feasts is known in
Judaism as the counting of the omer. An omer is a measure
of barley, and every day an omer was measured out and
they would count out, "day one of the counting of the
omer" until they came to the 50th day, Shavuot. On this
50th day, the barley harvest was complete and now the
wheat harvest would be offered before the Lord.

After Passover this year (2014), our close friend,
Daniel Schuman Kemp, said something to me that initiated
my realization that the omer count is a very special time.
He said something like, "At the end of every Passover
Seder, after their hearts are burning from the bridal reality
they just experienced in the third cup, it would be awesome
to cast a vision for the counting of the omer. You could
create an expectation that there is more! That it is
important to be like little kids counting the days until their
birthday... That in 50 days, the next appointment with Him
is coming, and it is about a marriage!! Wouldn't that be
awesome?!"

Of course I agreed, but I had never thought of that
before! Thirty-eight years of doing Passover and we always
finished the evening full of food, fun, and thankful for His
presence encountering hearts, but had never cast the vision
of what was next. Then it hit me. You cannot give what
you have not experienced yourself. I have not had much
heart connect to the counting of the Omer. However it's
interesting to note that it was during the same season, after
Jesus' resurrection, that He spent personal time with His

followers for forty days. During the last ten days of the Omer count, His disciples waited with anticipation in Jerusalem for "the promise of the Father". Now I am asking, and seeking Him to let me encounter Him in it, and next Passover, I will try to do exactly what Daniel suggested.

The Book of Ruth

It is traditional to read the book of Ruth on Shavuot. **Judges 1:22** says, ***"...they (Ruth and Naomi) came to Bethlehem at the time of barley harvest."*** The richness of this sentence is enormous. At an "appointed time", at the time of a "moed", when Israel was in physical and spiritual famine, God sends Ruth, a gentile girl to bring them hope.

Reuven Doran, a native Israeli believer, taught a message on the prophetic picture found in the book of Ruth that I will never forget. He said at a time of great darkness in Israel, when Naomi (representing Israel) was hopeless in her widowhood, being old, tired, childless and barren, God sent her provision. It came in a way she never could have imagined. Her Gentile daughter-in-law from Moab, also a widow, loved Naomi and followed her back to Bethlehem Judah. We all know the story how Ruth went to glean in the field of a Jewish man, Boaz, who noticed her, married her and became a kinsman redeemer to Naomi's family lineage. The child from Ruth and Boaz became the grandfather of King David whose bloodline brought the future Messiah. Reuven saw this as a picture of God sending a Gentile bride joined to a Jewish man and the Jewish nation and being the womb to bring forth the child (the first coming of Messiah) that Naomi (Israel) was unable to bear on her own. Likewise, Reuven said, it will also take a Gentile "womb of intercession" to come alongside Israel in the future to bring forth the second coming of Messiah.

The book of Ruth is such a powerful picture of a multifaceted reality. Israel married God on Mt. Sinai and in the midst of their time of unfaithfulness, He mercifully grafts in a Gentile servant girl from Moab to bring hope and redemption to His people. The book of Ruth is a glorious picture of what He always had in mind; a bride made up of Jews and Gentiles, one new man. Gary Weins says in his book, Bridal Intercession,

> **"This story, again historically accurate, stands as a prophetic illustration of the heart of God towards His people. The story is powerful in that it centers on God's embrace of Gentile people in his plans to find His Bride. It is one of the first pictures in the Scriptures demonstrating that relationship with God is established in the heart arena of faith, not within the confines of ethnic heritage."**
>
> **p. 29**

As a final note to this thought, it is important not to ever use the illustration found in Ruth as a way to justify the deceptive position that has plagued the church for 1800 years. Ruth is not a picture of a gentile bride replacing God's first bride, Israel. It is actually just the opposite. Rather it is a beautiful demonstration of what Romans 11 means for the Gentile believers to be grafted into an already existing olive tree. Through her marriage to Boaz, Ruth joined herself to a Jewish family, a Jewish culture, a Jewish nation, and their Jewish God. It is the same for all of us who come to know the Jewish Kinsman-Redeemer, Jesus.

The book of Ruth has a very personal meaning to me. It was through my marriage to John that I came to "glean" riches from a Jewish field, and it was through loving and caring for my Jewish mother-in-law for 31 years (my Naomi), that I learned their culture and perspective on life, and where I stumbled onto "Ruth's Road" and found the rich pattern of the festivals that God has been excited to reveal to those who love Him. In closing, I will share my journal entry from Shavuot, 2012.

Pondering on Shavuot, 2012

<u>Christie's Journal Entry</u>

"I thought of those 50 days in between the barley and the wheat harvests. Counting of the Omer... Countdown to something... something is building to a crescendo... Something is ready to breakout... Expectation at a mountain in Exodus 19... Jesus tells them to wait with expectation of something to happen... Wait in Jerusalem. We know what happens in the book of Acts... When Pentecost or Shavuot had fully come… God poured out the Holy Spirit... Just like when He brought the nation of Israel to Mount Sinai to enter into a marriage contract... But what happened during the counting of the Omer? What was God doing in the wilderness with His people to prepare a group of newly freed slaves to meet Him on a mountain? He was present with them every minute. He did not leave them for a second. It was not a time of silence. Similarly, what was Jesus doing from the time of His resurrection until the Shavuot?

209

He appeared to many for 40 days... the disciples, served dinner, cooked dinner on the beach... Road to Emmaus, and John says in His gospel that Jesus did so many things that all the books in the world could not contain the record of all the things that He did!! But why did He disappear in the clouds at 40 days? What is the pattern of the 10 days between the time that he ascended in the clouds and Shavuot? Interesting.

What message did Jesus send to His followers by His appearing those 40 days? It was though He was saying: "I am alive... I am present with you personally, and I care about the deep things of your heart... Thank you for following after Me, even when everything in the natural tried to defeat your faith... I remember the kindness of your youth, the love of your betrothal, when you went after me in the wilderness... You left all... gave up all... trusted Me when you have never even seen Me... thank you. You will not be disappointed. I know you cannot sustain yourself... I know you get discouraged... I know it seems like one big 'hope deferred' at times, but wait, keep trusting, keep walking through this barren wilderness where everything around you wants to say it is foolish to believe... that you are wasting your life... I am here... I am present... you will not be disappointed... thank you for your kindness in following after Me."

What is our heart posture today as we wait for this appointment? Remember, God just delivered a group of slaves with mighty signs and wonders out of an evil land and killed the one who held them captive. The Lord was more than a benevolent deliverer that felt sorry for His people... He was executing a plan that He, the Father and the Holy Spirit set in motion before the world was created. He was after a partner, a Bride and He was taking them somewhere. The next "moed" was under a bridal chuppah on a mountain and when God "proposed" all the nation of Israel said yes. Their identity changed from slaves to priests and kings then to a bride on a mountain. Why? Because He was reminding them of why He was coming in the future! To restore face to face relationship that He had in the garden.

The book of Ruth is a picture of the future Gentile bride being grafted in (Romans 11); a girl from a pagan culture who is a poor beggar after her husband's death, and becomes a redeemed mother of Israel that brought forth the future Messiah. Barley to wheat... Poor to rich... Forsaken and barren to married, chosen and fruitful... it is an amazing story, and it is ours!

Jesus was sown as the suffering servant Messiah into the ground during the Feast of Unleavened bread, and three days later was resurrected at the time of the First Fruits of the barley harvest (the poorest of crops), 49 days later (after the counting of the omer) the wheat crop came up (the richest crops). This is the Festival of Weeks or Shavuot, which He fulfilled by pouring out His spirit! From flat matzah at Passover to abundant loaves at Shavuot... what a great picture!

Jesus betrothed us in the upper room. He paid a bride price with His blood, and left a bride gift at Pentecost, His Holy Spirit in us! We have a legal bridal identity. The release of joy was bridal wine... An expression of how we are now to be living and carrying our heart. Mary of Bethany, relational heart. She was the wise virgin... Martha was the foolish virgin who lived out of issues, theology and doing... instead of devotional, sitting at His feet. It is not a contrast between righteous and wicked, but between wise and foolish. Being in love automatically makes us wise, because we become lovesick." -
End of journal entry-

Conclusion

On Shavuot, 2000 years ago, Jesus poured out His Spirit as the gift for His bride so she would have a deposit of Himself until He returned for her. He is right now interceding for us and building that heavenly bridal chamber that He will take us to when the Father says it is ready. Jesus perfectly fulfilled the pattern of the former rain spring feasts that Moses walked out in the book of Exodus and then wrote down in Leviticus 23; the very feasts that the Jewish people have been faithfully rehearsing and observing for 3500 years. I will never forget the day this revelation hit my heart. I can even remember where I was sitting that very moment when I said to Him, "If you fulfilled the spring pattern so perfectly, that means that you will come the second time according to the pattern of the fall feasts!!"

Hidden in Leviticus 23, a portion of scripture that is briefly read and often seen as that boring, legalistic Jewish stuff, is the actual blueprint of His first and second coming! In 38 years, I only have a tiny glimpse of what I know is valuable treasure waiting to be discovered. In the last six years I have had more of an awareness of the second coming of Jesus and the revelation of the fall feasts is coming at me faster than I can even begin to process. I certainly will not be so bold to say that I have anything figured out.

The fall feasts are prophetic, unchartered waters that can only be navigated with the humility and awe of a child-like heart that is looking to know Him and encounter Him. Any conclusions we come up with will be puny in comparison to the storyline that God has written and will soon begin to unfold! The grand finale to this age of history will be a dramatic, epic screenplay that we will be talking about for an eternity. But as it is written: ***"Eye has not seen, nor ear heard, Nor have entered into the heart of man The things which God has prepared for those who love Him." (1 Cor. 2:9).***

So it is with awe and reverence, along with child-like anticipation that I will next share my journey that I have had all these years walking with Jesus in the latter rain, fall feasts. I want you to stay with me on "Ruth's Road" so I will throw out a few things to build your expectations. In the rites and ceremonies given to Moses and kept alive by Jewish people all these years we find: a wedding of the Messiah, a coronation of the King of Kings, a last trump, an understanding of the Book of Life, a time called Jacob's trouble, a Day of Judgment, and much more. In short, a Bridegroom, King and Judge!

"Let us know, Let us pursue the knowledge of the LORD. His going forth is established as the morning; He will come to us like the rain, Like the latter and former rain to the earth."

Hosea 6:3

"Bridegroom of love, awaken my heart, Let me feel the passion that's burning in You. Bride of your choice, how can it be? The mystery of ages, how that You've chosen me."

Daniel Brymer

~ Chapter 7 ~

The Sabbath: The Final Destination

"Every Sabbath the Jews pre-enact the coming of messianic restoration. For a day, the sounds of joy and gladness, the voice of the groom and the bride, reverberate in the streets of a restored Zion. For 25 hours the heavenly Jerusalem exists on earth...in France, and Poland, in Yemen and Bombay. No wonder when the road to the earthly Jerusalem opened up, there were Jews who knew exactly what to do and where to go"
Rabbi Irving Greenberg

I have left the Sabbath for the last chapter on purpose. Like the other appointed times, I have had much personal history with God, looking for His heart of understanding and revelation pertaining to this mysterious day that in Genesis 2:3, God blesses and sets aside as holy. One day out of all other days, He intentionally makes a distinction. What is He saying? Why is He emphasizing this day in the account of the creation? Before the fall of man, before sin enters to defile and destroy, He proclaims a Day. Why?

As you have read through Leviticus 23 with me where all His appointed feasts are mentioned, did you notice what took me at least 20 years to see? Did you wonder why the first "moed" listed was the Sabbath? Before the spring and fall pattern of His first and second comings, he inserts this day that stands by itself, at the very beginning of the list, declaring its importance. It is proclaimed as something to rehearse because He calls it a "holy convocation", (rehearsal) like the others in Leviticus 23. It is to be rehearsed more often than any others... not just one time a year, but one time a week! It must be very important. But it is not part of the pattern of the other feasts. It is not one of the steps of the Messiah's rescue plan to redeem His bride. What, then, is it?

My Journey Into the Sabbath

We often would go to John's parents' house for Sabbath (or "Shabbos" as it is pronounced by most European Jews). Usually by the time we arrived at their home, the Sabbath candles were lit on the dining room table, the challah (a large, braided loaf made special for Sabbath) was on the table with a challah cover, and the glass of Sabbath wine was ready to drink. There was no special attention directed towards these things during the evening, other than everyone eating a piece of challah and drinking the wine and saying, "Good Shabbos". But, for some strange reason, when I walked in their home on Friday nights to see their table set for a special dinner and saw the Sabbath candles burning, I felt the presence of the Lord beckoning me to come and find Him.

I was curious, but did not pursue Him in the Sabbath at that time. I was focused on the appointed times of the festivals and the Sabbath just seemed to stand alone unconnected. Since I was not pursuing Him in it, He

216

decided to sneak up on us and gave us a taste of this holy day that John and I still savor. ***Proverbs 22:6*** says, ***"Train up a child in the way he should go, And when he is old he will not depart from it."*** A Hebrew commentary on this word "train" said it means to give a taste of something so good, the child will not forget. It is the reason for putting honey on a Jewish toddler's tongue when he begins the study of God's word. It is a reminder that His Word is sweet. This is what God did to give us our first taste of the Sabbath. He wanted us to know that this day holds substance and encounter so we would not dismiss its significance.

For some reason, many times God gives John and I the experience of something before the understanding. I fell in love with the person of Jesus and decided to follow Him before I knew I needed to be saved. I understood the doctrine of salvation later. When John and I were baptized in the Holy Spirit, we did not know there was such an experience. We went to a small group at the Denver Vineyard Church and said if there wasn't more to the Christian faith than what we had at the time, we were not going to make it. They seemed to know what we needed and prayed for us to be baptized in the Holy Spirit. We went home that night totally different but did not understand doctrinally what had happened to us until later.

Deliverance in water baptism was the same way for me. When John and I were new Christians, we were water baptized because we were told that it was important to identify with the death, burial and resurrection of Jesus. Five years later I was tormented with recurring dreams from my non-believing past. I prayed desperately for Him to set me free and then He said, "bury it in baptism". There was a new believer's baptism coming up the next Sunday at church and He was telling me to be part of it. I argued that I had already been baptized and it was unnecessary, but I was so desperate to get free from the nightly torment disrupting my sleep, that I humbled myself and got in the baptism line that next Sunday. I came up out of those waters totally set free from dreams and the torment! What had just happened to me? It did not fit into my church doctrine. It was not for another 10 years before the understanding came when the Lord taught me about the power of deliverance in the third cup of redemption during Passover that disarms principalities and powers. My experience with the Sabbath was the same.

How We Stumbled Into the Sabbath "Accidentally"

About 1984, we were living in Loveland Colorado and John had the desire to open our home up on Friday nights to anyone that wanted to come. He felt we were to worship together, take communion, and pray. A small group of people came regularly from different churches around our city, and some from towns further away. Our friend Tim Ruthven, would come also whenever he was not away teaching somewhere. One particular Friday night, as John was praying over the bread and wine, something unusual started to happen. We all started feeling the presence of the Lord, and John began sensing Him wanting us to enter into something that He was doing. John said, "I feel the Lord wants us to take communion for ourselves first, and then a second time for someone in the world who is being persecuted for their faith." One by one, people in the group began seeing faces of people to pray for. I saw a picture of a man and his wife in an Asian country crying, so I took a piece of bread and drank some wine and prayed that as I did, God would fill them with faith and hope. John saw a man in Eastern Europe in a prison cell and took the wine and bread and prayed for the strength of the Holy Spirit to fill him. The man's face that John saw was so real to him, that to this day, 25 years later, John still takes communion twice; once for himself, and once for the Christian man that he saw in that vision.

The Friday after that was the same. John lifted the bread and wine to pray and we waited for a few minutes, asking the Holy Spirit what He wanted to do. The presence of the Lord came again, and this time John saw Jesus stretched across our table saying He had abundant life for us and to eat more of Him. We would pass the bread around and then John felt Him say, "More, eat more of Me". So we kept passing this huge loaf of bread around the table, eating the bread, and as we did, waves of His presence would come. We ate the whole loaf and we felt He wanted to show us that He was much more than a meager little crumb of bread; He wanted us to live with an abundant expectation of Who He was and what He could do.

Each week was something new and different and as we waited on Him, His presence would come. One Friday, late afternoon, I went to the store to get bread and then next door to the liquor store to get wine for communion. The atmosphere in the liquor store was T.G.I.F, "Thank God It's Friday, now we can party!" I smiled to myself thinking how funny it was that I was in line to get my wine, but we were excited about a totally different kind of party! As I was walking to my car, I felt the Lord say, "Thank you for honoring this special, holy time. There are very few in this city who are entering into this day with Me."

I sat in my car stunned for a minute. What holy time, what special day were we entering into? Then I remembered the candles, the bread and the wine on John's parents' table that were always there to honor the Friday night Sabbath. I suddenly got it. Unintentionally, every Friday night, we were entering into the Sabbath. We had no idea, but I suddenly understood why He came with His presence each week. He was wanting us to look for Him in the mystery of this "moed", appointment, and He "allured" us (Hosea 2:14) to follow Him because we so loved Him showing up and being with us. Then one Friday it seemed that He just stopped coming.

We lit our candles, invited Him to be with us, passed the bread and wine, but felt nothing. We continued for a while in faith, knowing that you can't go by feelings, but we were ruined and without Him "doing" the Sabbath felt dead and religious. So, we quit. After that we put the Sabbath on a shelf, knowing it held true substance, but we lacked understanding of the meaning behind it. We would still light our candles and have challah and wine set out to take communion but we did not want to artificially work something up. All we knew was that it was an important picture of something close to God's heart, and for quite a few years, we left it at that.

Over the years, because people knew that we hosted Jewish festivals, they would ask us to "do the Sabbath" with them. I love celebrating the Sabbath as a special evening with friends and family to gather around. It is always good to eat a meal together and have fellowship in the word and take communion together, but I often sensed they were asking for a guaranteed experience with the Lord in it. I know we had a sovereign visitation with Him in the past, but we cannot make that happen again because it was nothing that we "did". He was just gracious for a time to bless us with His presence. However, it is His weekly appointment, and it is something we like to honor Him in because we know it is special, and we believe He is blessed by those who acknowledge this day and enter into the powerful prophetic picture that it proclaims. What is the prophetic picture? After 39 years of asking Him to give me revelation knowledge of this day and unlock the mysteries that the Sabbath holds, I think I am beginning to see something amazing, but it is still only a glimpse.

The Sabbath is a Place

In 2010, sitting in The International House of Prayer in Kansas City, I was enjoying a worship set and God dropped a random word into my heart. He said, "The Sabbath is a place". Not really understanding what He was saying, I wrote it down, knowing it was a significant revelation and have pondered it in my heart ever since. Over the years I had read things about the Sabbath from the writings of Jewish men and women who seemed to grasp something almost mystical about this day.

Rabbi Irving Greenberg in his book, The Jewish Way, has helped me get an overview of the core value of redemption woven through the festivals. His writing on the Sabbath has aided me in seeing a glimpse into a revelation that is finally beginning to unfold. There is a saying that I have read in several Jewish books that, "more than the Jews kept the Sabbath, the Sabbath kept the Jews". It kept them walking through 6,000 years of a history that has been riddled with oppressors, hardship and near annihilation. It is an absolute miracle that they are still a distinct people. What kept them unified and gave them the strength and the will power to keep going and not assimilate and give up? The answer is the Sabbath. There is a clue to that answer that caught my attention a few years ago found in Isaiah.

> **"If you turn away your foot from the Sabbath, From doing your pleasure on My holy day, And call the Sabbath a delight, The holy day of the LORD honorable, And shall honor Him, not doing your own ways, Nor finding your own pleasure, Nor speaking your own words, Then you shall delight yourself in the LORD; And I will cause you to ride on the high hills of the earth, And feed you with the heritage of Jacob your father. The mouth of the LORD has spoken."**
>
> **Is. 58:13**

Instead of the image that many Christians have of a legalistic, religious burden in keeping the Sabbath and festivals (which can happen when practiced under the wrong spirit), this verse is saying just the opposite. The Lord is saying we can have joy and pleasure when we delight in his appointments. This got my attention, especially because I can testify to the fact that the only reason I have kept walking through the pattern of the feasts these past 39 years is because I found pleasure and delight with Him as I did! Without His presence, the revelation of Jesus, the

The Lord is saying we can have joy and pleasure when we delight in his appointments.

fellowship with the Holy Spirit, and feeling the pleasure of the Father, I would have quit years ago.

The Mystery of the Sabbath

So what is it in the Sabbath that has kept the Jews? The answer is simple. He made it pleasurable; He made it alive for those who would keep it with Him and not make it a religious duty, but see it as a gift that their Bridegroom gave to a group of redeemed slaves who worked seven days a week for 430 years. Now let's see if we can begin to unwrap the contents of this special gift called Sabbath.

Rabbi Greenberg says, **"The Shabbat is the foretaste of messianic redemption" (The Jewish Way, p. 129).** He goes on to say,

> **"The power of the rhythm of redemption is that it allows the fullest participation in the world as it is, while giving recurrent fulfillment to the ultimate dreams of perfection. This periodic taste of fulfillment became the protection against the bitterness of gratification indefinitely postponed. Every seven days, the people of Israel were 'married' again to the Divine lover and the beloved Shabbat queen. On Friday night, Jews sing a special Shabbat prayer-poem, Lecha Dodi: 'Come my beloved to greet the bride, the Shabbat...'. By this expression of weekly marriage and consummation with the Lord, the people Israel was protected from**

being the eternal pining lover whose capacity for real love shrivels up in longing kept permanently within"

Once a week they rehearse the weekly, "holy convocation" (rehearsal, Leviticus 23:2) to keep the "moed", or "appointment" on God's calendar. That is why the Sabbath is listed first in Leviticus 23, because it is a

The Sabbath is a place.

rehearsal of the destination. The spring and fall festivals that follow are the steps the Messiah Jesus will walk through in His first and second comings to get us to that destination. The Sabbath is the goal. The Sabbath, He has now revealed to me, is the Garden of Eden restored. The Sabbath is a place. We are to be living as co-redeemers with Him; living as participants in His plan of redemption to "go about doing good" like Jesus, and bringing life, healing, wholeness and light to our sphere of influence for as long as we live. We are to be living in partnership with Him, as His bride, taking redemption to our generation as far as we can so we can pass the baton of this mandate to the next generation that follows until that Day when He returns to finish the job and cleanse the earth. Then the Father's throne can once more come down to Paradise restored and He can finally get what He paid for: a place to dwell in intimacy with us. Every Friday night we celebrate the 7,000-year plan of God from Genesis.

"Thus the heavens and the earth, and all the host of them, were finished. And on the seventh day God ended His work which He had done, and He rested on the seventh day from all His work which He

had done. Then God blessed the seventh day and sanctified it, because in it He rested from all His work which God had created and made."

Gen. 2:1-3

The Jewish people see in this the seven thousand year plan of God: 6,000 years and then the 7,000th year begins the eternal Sabbath, called the "Ha Ba Olam", the age to come. So what is the "rehearsal" we are to keep alive every Friday at sundown until Saturday at sundown? We light our candles proclaiming that Jesus is the light of this

> *We sanctify time and step into a place called the Sabbath*

dark world; we take communion to remind ourselves that He initiated a betrothal ceremony with us the night before He died when He took that cup of wine and the bread (the afikoman) after dinner at the Passover Seder. He said He was going to prepare a place for us to dwell with Him, which means He is coming back for us; We sanctify time and step into a place called the Sabbath and by so doing we are proclaiming before principalities and powers and all of heaven that there is a Day coming when evil and darkness will be no more and this world will be paradise once again; we proclaim the crowning age to come called, "the day of His wedding, the day of the gladness of His heart". (SOS 3:11). We rehearse it, we proclaim it, and we celebrate with Him weekly this glorious Day so that we don't forget where we are going and we keep the vision alive in our hearts.

Focusing on the Destination

I read in a Jewish book a story of a Rabbi who met a tightrope walker in a Russian prison and learned a valuable lesson from him. The Rabbi asked him what the secret of his art was; was it learning balance and concentration? The tightrope walker's answer was neither. He said the secret was keeping your eyes always on the destination. He said the hardest, most dangerous part is not in the middle, but rather when you make the turn. He said in that fraction of a second when you can no longer see your destination you are most likely to fall.

> *when you can no longer see your destination you are most likely to fall*

I believe that is true for us also. The patterns of the festivals on His calendar are His appointments in His appointment book. He wants us to keep them (rehearse them) with Him and proclaim them (invite people to come). Meeting with Him throughout the year we are remembering that He saved us out of this world under Satan's dominion, and that He is always present to save us from any bondage in our lives that He has already paid for. Each year we remember that we were taken out of the world for more than salvation, but for deliverance from our old identity as slaves, in order to rejoice in our new identity as a betrothed people that He is one day coming back for.

In the spring feasts we rejoice and keep alive what He has already done for us and in the fall feasts we see a glorious pattern of a Judge, a conquering King, and a High Priest that is coming out of a bridal chamber to remove evil from the earth and take His rightful reign as King of Kings on the earth. Proclaiming the weekly Sabbath and entering into a day as though it was here already, keeps the

226

destination always in our sights. We remember who we are and where we are going. However, God knows it has to have "substance" to experience Him in order to keep us motivated to keep going.

Proclaiming the truths is not enough. When we keep His appointments with child-like hearts, expecting Him to come, we may not always "feel" His presence, but we can be assured that He is in our midst and He is pleased. Rebbetzin Esther Jungreis says this about the Sabbath in her book, The Committed Life:

> **"...the Sabbath is a special gift hidden in God's treasure house. If we embrace the Sabbath, if we allow the Sabbath to take hold of our lives, then God lifts us up and invites us up and invites us into His private chambers, and so every Sabbath that is truly observed is a 'taste of the world to come." (p.290)**

If you see the movie "Fiddler on the Roof", there is a special scene where you watch as his family transitions from their poor, mundane life, to suddenly being in frantic preparation to be ready for the Sabbath at sundown. They treat the time approaching as a special guest they are getting ready to greet. They change into their finest clothes and the table is beautifully set with special foods prepared. They gather around the table, light the Sabbath candles and the atmosphere becomes transformed with a heavenly glow. Their home is no longer the humble dwelling of Tevia the milk man, but Tevia the king. They sing and welcome God's presence and ask for His blessing on their household. They leave one world behind and step into an alternate reality.

Because it is a picture of the messianic redemption to come when all things are perfect and paradise is once more dwelling under God's rule on earth, the goal is to create an atmosphere of total peace where problems and stress no longer exist and there is only a community dwelling intimately together in joy and in activities that are pleasurable. Complaining, harsh words and bad attitudes are not allowed. They strive to obey *Isaiah 58:13* that commands us *"to call the Sabbath a delight (oneg), and to honor God's holy day"(paraphrased)*.

Rabbi Greenberg says,

"The Shabbat is honored by anticipation, preparation, special dress, cleaning, washing, and personally participating in the creation of the atmosphere. The delight of Shabbat is experienced through good food and drink, adequate meals, a joyful mood, communal song and dance, peace (no fighting on Shabbat), intimacy and sexual relations. All cares should be put aside. Learning when heaven and liturgical experiences provide a spiritual dimension to 'honor' and 'delight'. Participating in this weekly rehearsal of the age to come, when heaven comes to earth, and the King of the universe takes

His rightful throne, keeps our destination constantly alive and reminds us of what our lives are about and where we are going."

The Jewish Way, p. 164

"Where there is no vision, the people perish..."

Prov. 29:18(KJV)

What began in a Garden will end in a Garden. It explains why Judaism does not mention heaven as our final destination. Earth is their given assignment to redeem with the Messiah so that one day heaven can come down and be restored to Sabbath rest. The culmination of human history is a perfect bridal people dwelling together with God on the earth forever. In the meantime, there is still work to be done before the Father's throne can come down to earth. There are still some "moedim", appointments, left on the biblical calendar for Jesus to fulfill that signal a time the Jewish people refer to as "Jacob's trouble". In the next book I will share with you the language of these fall festivals written throughout our Bible. When you put the overlay of these feasts on top of the end time scriptures, you will be astounded at what will begin to come into focus. Not that our view of the final chapters of human history will ever measure up to the spectacular reality that they will actually be, but they definitely offer an exciting glimpse into what is to come.

The Rhythm of the Feasts

The rhythm of the "appointed times" listed in Leviticus 23 are the "river banks" that keep us walking in community, with each other and with God, celebrating with Him the miracle of His redemptive, bridal love. The festivals and the Sabbath are landmarks every year to keep us aware of where we have been, where we are in the present, and to keep us focused on where we are going in the future. They remind us that it is not only His story, but that we have been caught up in this prophetic story as well. His weekly and yearly appointments are invitations to come celebrate and feast with Him to encounter His heart and to be with Him where He is. He bids us to come and "taste and see" for ourselves, and to continually seek Him for another glimpse into the glorious unveiling of Himself. He is now and forever will be, the Afikoman, and I invite you on the journey to find Him.

I am including a picture of what I call my "kindergarten chart" in **Appendix A**. It took me almost 40 years to get this simple picture but I believe anything that cannot be explained simply enough for a 5 year old to understand, is not worth knowing. This chart will make more sense after you read, ***Watching and Waiting: Discovering Jesus in the Fall Feasts***, it's a simple overview of the pattern of the feasts that first Moses walked through and then 1500 years later, Jesus did too. The main thing I want you to see for now is that the divine romance that started in a garden will end in a garden after Jesus and His bride come to dwell on earth. In that glorious Day, all things will be redeemed and perfect once more. This place, this Paradise on earth, is called the Sabbath.

Blessed are You, Lord our G-d, the sovereign of the world, who created joy and celebration, bridegroom and bride, rejoicing, jubilation, pleasure and delight, love and brotherhood, peace and friendship. May there soon be heard, Lord our G-d, in the cities of Judea and in the streets of Jerusalem, the sound of joy and the sound of celebration, the voice of a bridegroom and the voice of a bride, the happy shouting of bridegrooms from their weddings and of young men from their feasts of song. Blessed are You, Lord, who makes the bridegroom and the bride rejoice together.

The seventh blessing of a Jewish wedding

~ Conclusion ~

Where Do We Go From Here

"When the Lord brought back the captivity of Zion, We were like those who dream. Then our mouth was filled with laughter, and our tongue with singing..."
Psalm 126:1-2

My prayer is that after reading this book, you realized that the content did not come from a lifetime of study, but rather, a search to find His heart. My search is ongoing, and with each festival, with each Sabbath, and with every scripture I read, I am asking the Father to reveal Jesus to me. I pray that if your own heart is stirred to keep searching for Him in the pattern of the Leviticus 23 festivals, that you do not feel overwhelmed if you are at the beginning of the journey. It has taken me almost 40 years to make a switch from Greek to Hebrew thinking and to plow through endless books the Holy Spirit put in my path to glean; sometimes only one sentence, and then toss away the rest.

I asked Him endless questions and sometimes He would take years to answer, or He would randomly drop things in my heart that I had never even thought to ask Him. My tenacity was fueled by the pleasure of His fellowship and presence in the pursuit, without which I never would have continued. So please don't feel overwhelmed. He will help you navigate through the foreign culture, the foreign thinking, and the Jewish concepts and idioms that are found throughout the Old and New Testaments. Yes, it will be foreign to your Greek lens that you have been looking through, but it is what He has grafted you into; He will give you revelation understanding and walk with you and be your teacher. Just stay child-like and don't focus on theology; focus first on His heart and His emotions, and your theology will follow. Bill Johnson from Redding California has a phrase, "Let my ceiling be your floor". So let my story, my testimony of what I have discovered this far, be your starting point. I guarantee in another 40 years, what I have discovered will seem elementary in comparison to what He is going to unfold to His Jewish and non-Jewish believers in these days.

After I finish teaching at various groups, I always get the same questions: "What books do you recommend?" It is always a hard question to answer because there are so many books that I would not recommend. I might have found one sentence in some of them that God highlighted to me and then told me to throw out the rest. Also, there are books that I might recommend to mature believers who have a solid relationship with God in His word, because they can "spit and chew" and discern what is from God's heart and lines up with scripture; but here is the problem. The writers of many of the books are Jewish men and women who have not yet had an encounter with Jesus as their Messiah. They are scholars, philosophers, and Rabbis, some of which, have a close relationship with God, but it is easy to see the life that Judaism offers and shift our attention away from Jesus as being the central focus of what everything is about.

I have seen new and seasoned believers get caught up in the love of Israel and Judaism and leave their faith in Jesus. Therefore, I do not want to take the chance of recommending a book that will be a stumbling block to anyone. However, one book that has been an absolute treasure in helping me see the Jewish mandate of redemption, as well as a valuable resource in understanding the heart and rhythm of life found in the biblical feasts, is Rabbi Irving Greenberg's book called The Jewish Way. I also gained further insights into the heart of Jewish life and perspective reading Rebbetzin Esther Jungries' book, The Committed Life. And lastly, the books by Abraham Joshua Heschel contain pearls of wisdom and a depth that mines the heart and soul of what it is to stand in awe and reverence of a holy God.

As the merging of Jew and Gentile progresses to more than a mental assent of being one new man like Ephesians 2 and 3 says, and the church of Jew and Gentile enters into the practical expression of this in the way we live and express our faith together, we will see many more books written. When the foundations of Jewish understanding and rites and ceremonies combined with the meaning of Jewish idioms found in the Bible come together with the revelation that it is all about Jesus, we are going to see a reformation of the church that is more powerful than the reformation of the 1500's under Martin Luther. It will not be legalistic and burdensome. We have yet to see the expression of what it will look like. This coming reformation will change the face of both Judaism and

Christianity, and will be what Paul in **Romans 11** calls, *"Life from the dead"*.

The second question I always get asked after I finish sharing is, "How do we begin walking in this?" My answer is simple. Just say yes and tell Him you want to find Him in the riches of the pattern of His festivals. With a child-like spirit and a resistance to gaining head knowledge before heart revelation, you are headed in the right direction. **Hebrews 11:6** tells us, *"...He is a rewarder of those who diligently seek Him."*

I am putting a workbook together named, *"**Rehearsing with Ruth:** The Journey Begins"* of some practical ways for you to begin celebrating the Sabbath and the festivals that will be available soon. Of course it will never be complete because it is an ongoing walking with Him, and there will be more riches to be unveiled for eternity. I will just give you some practical resources that John and I have done to get you started, and over time, you and the Holy Spirit will add your own unique expression and make it yours. We hope to form an international community walking out the biblical feasts together so we are creating a website, **ruthsroad.org**, as a place to post teachings and insights with one another to keep learning and celebrating together.

The website will keep you informed of new material we will publish in the future as well as short podcasts of new teaching material. We hope you come along with us... it is sure to be a rich and rewarding journey.

"And you will seek Me and find Me, when you search for Me with all your heart."
> **Jer. 29:13**

Looking Ahead

My husband John wanted me to include the preface of my next book; ***Watching and Waiting: Discovering Jesus in the Fall Feasts***. He said it so stirred his heart when I read it to him, that he wanted me to share it with you and help you anticipate the next part of our journey together.

Preface

In recent years there has been a growing hunger in the church to study end time events. As new believers, John and I had a vague understanding of the end-time rapture that was taught in the 1970's, but for the most part, the topic of the second coming of Jesus was rarely discussed. However, as my search for Jesus in the biblical feasts continued through the decades, my curiosity about His return to the earth increased. After years of gazing at the spring feasts and being unequivocally convinced that Jesus perfectly walked out every minute detail of the Leviticus 23 pattern, I have become equally convinced that He will keep the precise pattern of the fall feasts as well.

If you read my testimony of how the Holy Spirit led me on a treasure hunt through the spring feasts to help me encounter the heart of Jesus, you know my focus was centered more on knowing Him intimately than becoming a theological scholar. The same holds true as I attempt to share my insights into His second coming that is undeniably seen in the language and pattern of the fall festivals. I am not interested in debating end-time positions of "pre-trib, mid-trib, or post-trib". I am not looking to be "right". I am looking for burning hearts that want to have fellowship looking for Him in the mysteries of His Word, and the language of His festivals that give valuable clues to His future plan of redemption. I don't have theological conclusions that are set in stone. I have forty years of "ponderings" and questions that are ongoing between me and the Lord and a lot of, "Wow! What if this and what if that". I have journals with revelations to my heart that have sustained me and strengthened me to keep going and to keep seeking Him and that have made me love Him more. I am not finished with this journey but feel He has asked me to "quarah" (Leviticus 23:2), "proclaim and invite people to come", to join my search for Jesus the Afikoman, the Satisfaction, with me. I want child-like hearts that are not looking to "own" private knowledge that others do not have so they can start a ministry. That is a dangerous and prideful response to truth without the guidance of the Spirit of Truth. In the end it is not what you know but Who you know that matters. I feel a holy fear of the Lord to pray that my teaching leads to renewed intimacy with Jesus more than knowledge about Him. If that is your focus as you read this then I believe you will be blessed.

Because we are living in a generation that truly could be alive for His return to the earth, the Holy Spirit is stirring our hearts to search the scriptures as to how these events will unfold. When people hear that I teach on the biblical festivals they usually ask me to start by sharing the fall feasts because they are the prophetic feasts yet to be fulfilled. I understand why they want to get to the feasts that are relevant for today, but it is impossible for me to share the end of the story without the beginning. It is like Christians who were taught that it is unnecessary to read the Old Testament because it is not relevant for today; yet the New Testament does not make sense on its own. It is a continuation of everything that came before and it is the end of the story without the beginning and the middle!

The Bible is an epic love story and the main theme is the redemption of a Bride for the Father's Son and the restoration of a place for them to dwell together, redeeming the earth side by side so the earth can once more be presented to the Father and His throne can come down! In *1 Corinthians 15:20-28*, we see the focus where His glorious plan of redemption is ultimately headed:

> *"But now Christ is risen from the dead, and has become the firstfruits of those who have fallen asleep. For since by man came death, by Man also came the resurrection of the dead. For as in Adam all die, even so in Christ all shall be made alive. But each one in his own order: Christ the firstfruits, afterward those who are Christ's at His coming. Then comes the end, when He delivers the kingdom to God the Father, when He puts an end to all rule and all authority and power. For He must reign till He has put all enemies under His feet. The last enemy that will be destroyed is death. For "He has put all things under His feet." But when He says, "all things are put under Him," it is evident that He who put all things under Him is excepted. Now when all things are made subject to Him, then the Son Himself will also be subject to Him who put all things under Him, that God may be all in all."*

239

His plan of redemption is found in the Leviticus 23 feasts and they are connected to His Divine romance that unfolds from Genesis through Revelation. We need to stay connected to the whole story because it is glorious beginning to end! The feasts are not isolated "subjects" that stand alone. They are connected and only make sense when they are viewed like scenes from a screenplay that are rehearsed and lived out in real life. Rather than topics to be discussed in a seminary classroom, they are "shadows" (Colossians 2:16-17), and their substance is all about Him and what is in His heart for the Father and for His Bride!!!!

I have been looking for Jesus in the feasts since the first encounter I had with Him at my Jewish in-law's Passover meal forty years ago (see ***Finding the Afikoman: encounter Jesus in the spring feasts***, chapter 1). For 32 of those 40 years, I knew the Jewish understanding and ceremonial language of the fall feasts and celebrated them according to Jewish tradition. I even had encounters with Jesus in the doing of them. What I lacked was a Christian lens concerning the end times. Until John and I moved to Kansas City in 2008, we had never heard teaching from the Word on the second coming of Jesus. During a video teaching on the book of Revelation, I had a Holy Spirit encounter. The teacher was talking about a conquering King Jesus leading a glorious Bridal procession from Mt. Sinai to Jerusalem, and suddenly pictures and liturgy from the fall feasts started coming into focus. Pictures of things I had held in my heart concerning those feasts started to come to life! Suddenly portions of scripture from Ezekiel and Daniel, Isaiah, Zechariah and Joel had new perspective for me that lined up with the language of the feasts. Now eight years later, I am piecing more and more together and though there is a fuzzy picture still, it is much clearer than

240

it was eight years ago. In the second book, **_Watching and Waiting: Discovering Jesus in the Fall Feasts_** I will share with you my journey with Jesus through the fall feasts thus far, knowing that what I see is puny compared to the dramatic, real life fulfillment when He comes in the future.

Studying the fall festivals is like navigating uncharted waters. It is a prophetic pattern not yet fulfilled, so I would encourage a heart posture of finding His heart more than focusing on figuring it all out. The fall feasts are a script of an epic screenplay that will happen in real life with real people and a Man/God Who is coming to walk out the "grand finale" of all that has been in His heart from the beginning of time. This is NOT dead theology to engage your intellect, although your intellect will be satisfied. Rather, it is an opportunity to have fellowship with the Holy Spirit asking Him, "Where are you in this? Where is your heart? What are you feeling? What are you doing? What should Your people, Your bride, be doing right now?" Although I teach on the Jewish festivals, I do not just have a message. I have lived this message for 37 years. Abraham Joshua Heschel, a Jewish theologian said this in his book, I asked For Wonder:

> **"Everything depends on the person who stands in the front of the classroom. The teacher is not an automatic fountain from which intellectual beverages may be obtained. He is either a witness or a stranger. To guide a pupil into the Promised Land, he must have been there himself. When asking himself, 'Do I stand**

for what I teach? Do I believe what I say?', he must be able to answer in the affirmative." (pp. 87,88)

So I stand here before you as a witness. I have gazed at this Leviticus 23 pattern for 40 years and have asked the Lord to teach me and show me His heart. I know it may seem foreign and unfamiliar to you; I understand that. It is exactly why it took me 40 years to scratch the surface to get inside what I call the "Jewish box". The only way to "get it" is to respond to the invitation and walk with Jesus and ask the Holy Spirit to give you revelation of the Father's heart; but that is what it takes to understand any of the Word of God and to walk this journey of faith. So with that in mind, let's begin and crack open this mysterious, ancient door and with the Holy Spirit as our guide, let's begin our journey into the revelation of Jesus and His amazing end-time plan to come for His Bride.

"My heart is overflowing with a good theme; I recite my composition concerning the King; My tongue is the pen of a ready writer. You are fairer than the sons of men..."

Psalm 45:1

Connect With Us

There are two driving forces that make me keep rehearsing the biblical festivals each year. The first is feeling His pleasure and presence and the encounters that I experience as He reveals Jesus to my heart. The second is my desire to prepare a place for a community of believers to experience true fellowship as we do life, walking on His calendar together. I have always hoped that hosting the festivals for others would inspire them to want to start the journey themselves and that we could have a multitude of believers during the Feast of Tabernacles with succahs set up in their backyards; each with their own creative, individual expression with their own unique style. Can you imagine an international community with a childlike excitement gathering friends and family to these weekly and yearly celebrations and being able to post revelations and pictures of what they are doing and discovering as they walk this out? I can imagine the Father turning to His Son as they look down from heaven at the Feast of Tabernacles… seeing little succahs all over the earth with not only Jews but Jews and Gentiles alike, and hearing Him say: *"How lovely are your tents, O Jacob! Your dwellings, O Israel!" (Num 24:5).* My desire and I believe His, is to have a place to share ideas, revelations, recipes, and pictures with other believers around the world as they join us in walking this journey together.

If that is something you are interested in please stay connected with us in one of the following ways:

- **info@ruthsroad.org** -- Please send questions, comments or requests here

- **facebook.com/ruthsroadinc** -- Initially we will use this page to inform you about all things Ruth's Road.

- **ruthsroad.org** -- In 2016 we will have our website up and running to springboard more ways to connect

Through these three avenues we will announce upcoming events, share blogs, pictures, videos and much more in the near future. Thank you for your patience as we build the community links; no words can describe how excited we are to connect with you.

Bibliography

Irving Greenberg, <u>The Jewish Way: Living the Holidays</u>, New York, Summit Books, 1988

Rabbi Abraham J. Twerski, <u>From Bondage to Freedom</u>, New York, Sharr Press, 1995

Rebbetzin Esther Jungreis, <u>The Committed Life: Principles of Good Living From Our Timeless Past</u>, New York, HarperCollins Publisher, 1998

Andrew Jukes, <u>The Names of God in Holy Scripture</u>, Grand Rapids, Michigan, Kregel Publications, 1967

Gary Weins, <u>Bridal Intercession, Authority in Prayer through Bridal Intercession</u>, Greenwood, Missouri, Oasis House, 2001

Bob Sorge, <u>Power of the Blood: Approaching God with Confidence</u>,Greenwood, Missouri, Oasis House, 2008

Abraham Joshua Heschel, <u>I Asked For Wonder</u>, New York, The Crossroad Publishing Company, 1983

Note: The quote in Chapter 2, p.10 is taken from a Jewish source called the <u>Midrash Vayosha</u>. According to Wikipedia (wikipedia.org/wiki/midrash Vayosha), "The Midrash Vayosha is an 11th century C.E. smaller midrashim, based on Ex. 14:30-15: 18. It is an exposition the style of the later haggadah and seems to have been intended for 'Shabbat Shirah" or for the seventh day of Passover."
It was first published in Constantinople in 1519 and has been reprinted by:
A. Jellinek, Bet.Ha. Midrash i. 35-37, Jerusalem, 1967, 3rd edition

Appendix A:

<u>Divine Romance</u>

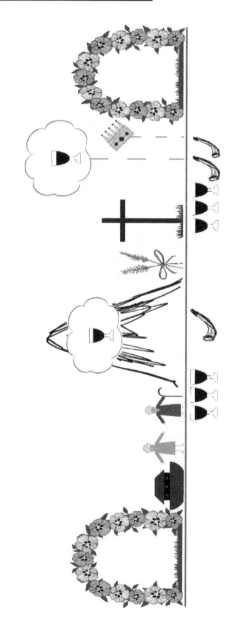

THE DIVINE ROMANCE

I carried this picture in my heart for years. One day I drove to Hobby Lobby, got a styrofoam board and some stickers and created what I call, "My Kindergarten Chart". I wanted a simple picture that even a five year old could understand. After 40 years of 'going deep' in the biblical festivals, this is my end product. John calls it my PHD thesis...

1. The Garden: Heaven on earth; God dwelling with man; walking together in intimate relationship

2. Noah's Ark: A righteous man saved from the flood in an ark of deliverance, while wrath was poured out on the wicked (the ark landed on Mt. Ararat on 17th of Aviv; First Fruits, the same day the children of Israel came up out of the Red Sea; the same day Jesus was raised from the dead)

3. Abraham: God found one man who was His friend; made covenant with him and promised that through his seed, all the nations would be blessed (becomes a family and goes to Egypt as 70 people; 430 years later; they leave as a nation)

4. Moses: He delivers the children of Israel out of Egypt (Exodus 12) according to the pattern found in Exodus 6: 6,7; the four cups of redemption:

   - Cup #1 - They cry out and He comes down

   - Cup #2 - The blood of a lamb covers them and 'takes' them out

   - Cup #3 - Redeemed: (bought back) from Pharaoh thru the Red Sea (baptism); free to become God's possession

- Cup #4 - Consummation: Moses brings them to Mt. Sinai 50 days later; betrothal (Exodus 19); 'marriage on the mountain'; Moses goes up; God comes down in a cloud

  - **1st Trump**: summoning a bride to the mountain

5. Wheat Stalk: calling of the Gentile bride; Ruth between barley and wheat harvest; foreshadowing of a Gentile bride being grafted in by marrying a Jewish redeemer

6. Jesus: Comes to earth and walks through the same pattern of redemption as Moses; becomes Passover Lamb

  - 3rd cup of betrothal: at Passover before He goes to the cross

  - Pays the 'bride price': with His blood

  - Leaves a 'gift' for His bride: Shavuot; the Holy Spirit (Acts 2)

  - Raised: goes to prepare a place to take them for consummation of marriage

7. Jesus coming with clouds: we meet Him in the air; clouds as chuppah (wedding canopy)

  - **Last Trump:** summons the bride

8. Conquering King: Jesus comes down with a bridal procession; comes to Jerusalem to rule on the earth with His bride

   - **Great Trump**: announcing bridal procession and judgment

9. The Garden restored to the earth: God's throne comes down to earth; intimacy restored; **SABBATH FOREVER!**

Appendix B:

Pattern of the Spring Feasts

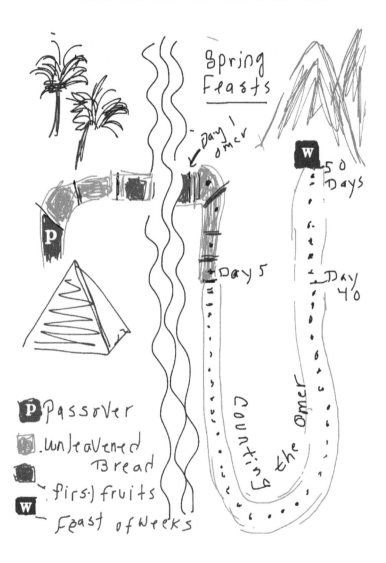

Spring Feasts

Day 1 omer

Day 5

50 Days

Day 40

Counting the Omer

P Passover

. unleavened Bread

- firstfruits

W - Feast of Weeks

This is chart shows the journey from Egypt to Mt. Sinai as the children of Israel walk through the pattern of the feasts.

Passover
- Children of Israel kill a lamb for their household and put the blood on their doorposts. They eat the lamb and prepare to leave Egypt that night.

Unleavened Bread
- They prepare provisions of unleavened bread because there was no time for it to rise. They plunder Egypt, leave sometime after midnight and there is none sick among them.

First Fruits
- Later known as the Barley harvest this is the day that the Children of Israel crossed the Red Sea all night and were raised on the other side the morning of the same day. (biblical day begins at sundown)

Counting the Omer
- It took 50 days to reach Mt. Sinai. During this time God showed them His abundant provision for them.

  Omer: a measure they were later told in Lev. 23 to count to give them an expectation for the next spring Feast of Shavuot. This is the 50 days between leaving Egypt and meeting with God at Mt. Sinai.

Shavuot/Pentecost
- The Children of Israel arrive at Mt. Sinai to enter into a marriage covenant with God. God comes down in cloud and Moses goes up to meet Him there.

Appendix C:

Fall Feasts

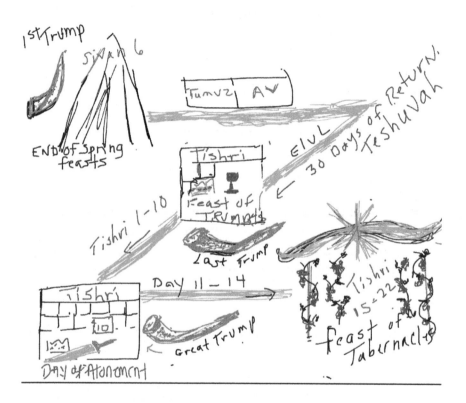

The chart begins at the last spring Feast of Shavuot, where the children of Israel enter into a covenant with God at Mt. Sinai. There are two months in between and then the month of Elul. After the 30 days of Elul, the fall feasts begin with the Feast of Trumpets and conclude with the Feast of Tabernacles. Elul is a time every year to prepare our hearts in anticipation of His return beginning at the first fall feast.

1. Feast of Trumpets / Rosh Hashanah
   - This is the first fall appointment and begins on Tishri 1.

   - These are the Jewish idioms and phrases that are traditionally associated with this feast.
     o Day of blowing the last trump
     o Resurrection of the dead
     o Day of Judgment
     o Day of Coronation of a King
     o Day of Wedding of the Messiah
     o Day of the Beginning of Jacob's Trouble
     o No man knows the day or hour
     o Open gates / open doors

Side Note: After Tishri 1 you will notice 10 more days of Teshuvah. This is an extended time of mercy for people to return to God. The 40 day time of Teshuvah commemorates the last 40 days when Moses went up on the mountain to plead God's mercy for the sin of the golden calf.

2. Yom Kippur or Day of Atonement is on Tishri 10
   - The most solemn day of the year, a day of fasting when the high priest goes in the holy of holies to make atonement for the nation and comes out declaring mercy

   - Gates are 'closed'; last chance to be written in the Book of Life

   - Conquering King returns to earth with His bride

3. Feast of Tabernacles is on Tishri 15-22
   - This is the last fall feast
   - It is 7 days long but it is so enjoyable that God added an extra day called the 8th day (not on the chart but listed in Lev. 23:36)
   - This is the most joyous feast of the year when they build temporary dwellings called booths and live in them for 7 days
   - Wedding feast?
   - Millennial Kingdom?
   - All nations celebrate (Zech. 14:16)

Appendix D:

Two Calendars / Two Theaters

I drew this chart to show the two theaters that are going on all the time. There is the theater in heaven where the Father and Jesus are governing their Kingdom and making preparations towards the future redemption of a people and a planet that they created. Then there is the theater on earth, where man has been walking through time since the day they were created and the world began. It is important to be aware that these two theaters are always alive and functioning. The one in heaven is focused on the events of redemption that began in the month of Aviv or Nissan, when God took His bride out of Egypt. The one on earth is doing "business as usual", walking through time since the book of Genesis and when the world was created on Tishri 1.

1. Heavenly Calendar: Nissan / Aviv
   - After Exodus 12:1 Nissan becomes the new first month of the year which is the beginning of God's courtship' with Israel

   - The clock starts ticking towards fulfillment of all Leviticus 23 appointments

2. Earthly Calendar: Tishri
   - Birthday of when the world was created

   - Where the kingdoms of this world plan their agendas

Appendix E:

Hebrew & Gregorian Calendar

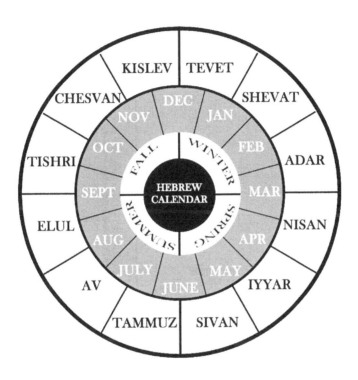

This chart gives you a visual of how the two calendars align with each other.

Appendix F:

This chart shows how the children of Israel walked out the pattern in the book of Exodus and then parallels how Jesus fulfilled it 1500 years later.

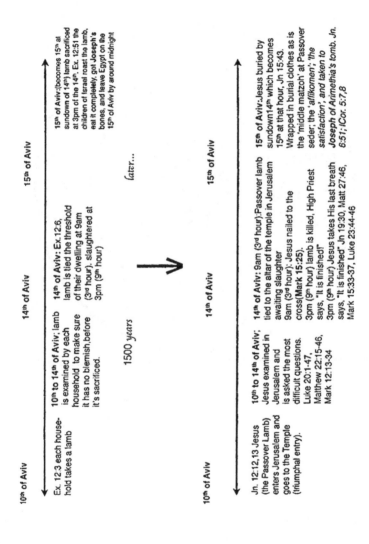

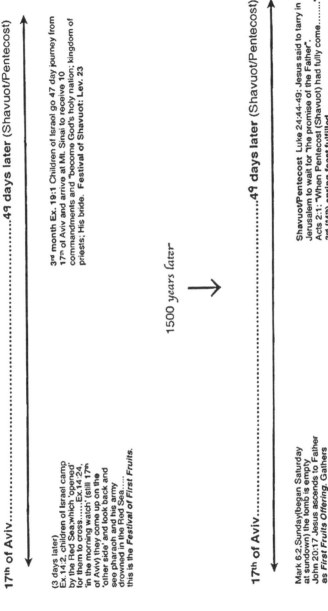

17th of Aviv.........................49 days later (Shavuot/Pentecost)

3rd month Ex. 19:1 Children of Israel go 47 day journey from 17th of Aviv and arrive at Mt. Sinai to receive 10 commandments and "become God's holy nation; kingdom of priests; His bride. Festival of Shavuot: Lev. 23

(3 days later) Ex.14:2, children of Israel camp by the Red Sea,which 'opened' for them to cross......Ex.14:24, 'in the morning watch' (still 17th of Aviv) they come up on the 'other side' and look back and see pharaoh and his army drowned in the Red Sea...... this is the *Festival of First Fruits.*

1500 *years later* →

17th of Aviv.........................49 days later (Shavuot/Pentecost)

Shavuot/Pentecost Luke 24:44-49: Jesus said to tarry in Jerusalem to wait for "the promise of the Father". Acts 2:1: "When Pentecost (Shavuot) had fully come......." 3rd ("4th") spring feast fulfilled

Mark 6:2,Sunday(began Saturday at sundown) the tomb is empty John 20:17 Jesus ascends to Father as *First Fruits Offering.* Gathers 'sheaves' of others whose graves were opened that day and were resurrected from the dead as 'first fruits'; and offering to the Father.

Appendix G:

The Goel

The members of the family in this wider sense had an obligation to help and to protect one another. There was in Israel an institution which defined the occasions when this obligation called for action; it is the institution of the goel, from a root which means 'to buy back or to redeem'; 'to lay claim to', but fundamentally its meaning is 'to protect'. The institution has analogies among other peoples (for example the Arabs). But in Israel it took a special form, with its own terminology.

The goel was a redeemer, a protector, a defender of the interests of the individual and of the group. If an Israelite had to sell himself into slavery in order to repay a debt, he would be 'redeemed' by one of his near relations (Lev. 25:47-49). If an Israelite had to sell his patrimony, the goel had priority over all other purchasers; it was his right and duty to buy it himself, to prevent the family property from being alienated. This law is codified in Lev. 25:25, and it was in his capacity as goel that Jeremiah bought the field of his cousin Hanamell (Jer. 32:6).

The story of Ruth is yet another illustration of this custom, but here the purchase of the land is rendered more complicated by a case of levirate. Naomi had some property, which, because of her poverty, she was forced to sell; and her daughter-in-law Ruth was a childless widow. Boaz was a goel of Naomi and Ruth (Ruth 2:20), but there was a closer relative who could exercise this right before him (Ruth 3:12; 4:4). This first goel would have bought the land, but he would not accept the double obligation of buying the land and marrying Ruth, because the child of this union would bear the name of the deceased husband and inherit the land (Ruth 4:4-6). To Boaz bought the family property and married Ruth (Ruth 4:9-10).

This story shows that the right of the goel followed a certain order o kinship, an order which is specified in Lev. 25:49; first the paternal uncle, then his son, then other relations. Further, the goel cold renounce his right or decline his duty without blame. By taking off one shoe (Ruth 4:7-8), a man proclaimed that he was forgoing his right; Duet. 25:9 describes a similar action in the law of levirate, but there the procedure is meant to bring the brother-in-law into disgrace. Comparison of this law with the story of Ruth seems to indicate that the obligation of the levirate was at first undertaken by the clan, like the redemption of the patrimony, but was later restricted to the brother-in-law.

One of the gravest obligations of the goel was blood-vengeance, but we have already examined this connection to tribal organization because it is rooted in desert custom.

The term goel passed into religious usage. Thus Yahweh, avenger of the oppressed and savior of His people is called a goel in Job 19:25; Ps 9:15; 78:35; Jer. 50:34 etc., and frequently in the second part of Isaiah 41:14; 43:14; 44:6,24; 49:7; 59:20, etc.).

Ancient Israel Vol. 1 by Roland de Vaux
Social Institutions pages 21-22

Appendix H:

Shavuot: What Happened on Mt. Sinai According to Jewish Tradition

The writings of Jewish Rabbi's and scholars are often a goldmine for finding parallels between the old and new testaments. The following quotes are taken from three different sources. Keep in mind that much of Jewish history and events were passed down orally from generation to generation. It is amazing how closely these accounts line up with *Acts 2,* ***"When the day of Pentecost (Shavuot) had fully come..."*** ***(Acts2:1)***

Rabbi Joseph Hertz says, "Revelation at Sinai, it was taught, was given in the desert territory, which belongs to no one nation exclusively; and it was not heard by Israel alone, but the inhabitants of all the earth. The *Divine Voice* divided itself in seventy tongues then spoken on earth, so that all the children of men might understand it's world-embracing and man-redeeming message... When God gave the torah on Sinai He displayed untold marvels to Israel with His voice. What happened? God spoke and the *Voice* reverberated throughout the world....It says, 'And all the people witnessed the thunderings.'" (1)

Another scholar, R. Johnson, said, "God's voice, as it was uttered, split up into seventy voices, in seventy languages, so that all the nations should understand. When each nation heard the *Voice* in their own vernacular, their soul departed (they were in fear), save Israel, who heard but were not hurt." (2) Ex: Rabbah 5.9

Rabbi Moshe Weissman comments on this significant event by saying, "On the occasion of *Matan torah* (the giving of the Torah), the *Bnai Yisrael* (the children of Israel) not only

262

heard *HaShem's* (the Lord's) *Voice,* but actually saw the sound waves as they emerged from *HaShem's* mouth. They visualized them as a fiery substance. Each commandment that left *HaShem's* mouth traveled around the entire camp and then came back to every Jew individually, asking him, 'Do you accept upon yourself this commandment with all the *halachot* (Jewish law) pertaining to it?' Every Jew answered, 'Yes', after each commandment. Finally, the fiery substance which they saw, engraved itself on the *luchot* (tablets)." (3)

1) Dr. Joseph Hertz, The Authorized Prayer Book, New York, Block Publishing, P, 791
2) Midrash, Exodus, Rabbah 5: 9
3) Rabbi Moshe Weissman, The Midrash Says on Shemot:, Benei Yakov pub. (1980) p. 182

Connect With Us

Once again, our heart is to have a place to share ideas, revelations, recipes, and pictures with other believers around the world as they join us in walking this journey together. If that is something you are interested in please stay connected with us in one of the following ways:

- **info@ruthsroad.org** -- Please send questions, comments or requests here

- **facebook.com/ruthsroadinc** -- Initially we will use this page to inform you about all things Ruth's Road.

- **ruthsroad.org** -- In 2016 we will have our website up and running to springboard more ways to connect

Upcoming Materials

Spring of 2016 – ***Rehearsing with Ruth:** **The Journey Begins***

Rehearsing with Ruth is a practical guide for those who desire to begin a personal journey into the feasts. John and Christie will share the way they have celebrated over the years with their family and friends to give you some ideas on how to get started as you find your own expression.

Winter of 2017 – ***Watching and Waiting:** **Discovering Jesus in the Fall Feasts***

This is a companion book to *Finding the Afikoman: encountering Jesus in the spring feasts.* Just as Christie led you through her encounters with Jesus in the spring feasts, the first coming of Jesus; likewise, she will share her 40 year journey with the fall feasts/second coming of Jesus.

264

Made in the USA
Monee, IL
06 September 2019